A THOROUGHLY MODERN
PLAYER PIANO

A FUN AND INTENSIVE
DO-IT-YOURSELF BUILDING PROJECT
DESIGNED TO TEACH THE BASICS OF
MUSIC, ROBOTS, ELECTRONICS AND
COMPUTER HARDWARE AND SOFTWARE

CHARLES A. MATHYS

Netcam Publishing
Naples, Florida

ISBN: 978-0-9843775-3-4 (1/2/17)
LCCN: PENDING

Contribution Acknowledgement
Inside Graphics/Photos: by the author unless otherwise indicated

Dedication

*For my son Steve who passed away during the creation
and development of this project. He wrote the original version of the
Arduino sketch which interprets and plays the notes.*

*Steve was a wonderful human being who did the best he could
to live a normal life considering the many devastating
adversities that his childhood diabetes caused.*

*I am so happy to have been able to spend so much time
with him and I am so thankful that he put his
brilliant mind to work on this project.*

Acknowledgements

I would like to thank the many people who helped me put this book together. Steve, wherever you are, I could not have done it without you.

My wife of 60 years, Marjorie, who lets me play with my computers instead of doing much more important tasks around the house and never complained about having had to listen to "Fur Elise" a few hundred times.

Many friends especially Bob McKelvey, George Gonser and Chuck Austin, who reviewed early manuscripts and provided many helpful ideas and suggestions.

My grandson Dan Robartes helped me with my PC problems, thought of the apps to solve some of our solenoid problems and reviewed the entire book. My granddaughter Kelley Mathys edited the entire manuscript. She corrected my grammar and was a great help putting the glossary together. My editor Peter Tuths who also reviewed the whole book and provided many helpful suggestions.

To Cheryl Sivewright who designed the cover and put the book together according to the printer's specifications, a very big thank you.

Preface

Player pianos attained the height of their popularity about 100 years ago. As the 20th century progressed, their demand decreased with the improvement of disk recordings and record players which were much less expensive and much simpler to operate. According to Arthur Reblitz, author of "Player Piano, Servicing and Rebuilding" in their heyday more player pianos were sold than uprights or grand pianos. Even today many seniors remember fondly their grand-parents' player piano complete with the piano rolls and the pedals that were pumped in order to play an old- fashioned tune.

This book is not about trying to revive those good old days but rather to explore the idea of "live" entertainment that can be produced with our new technology. There is something truly fascinating about watching the mini-robots operating in sequence and generating music. For the musically gifted, a favorite piece can be re-arranged to his taste or a new tune can be created without the finger dexterity and the many years of practice that are required to play the piano correctly. For guitar players needing a bit of help with the melody, this is a fine way to practice as a duo. With the accompaniment options available in the keyboard, a trio might even be formed!

My main goal in this book is to provide a powerful learning experi-ence by describing an exciting project that can be used to gain familiarity with sheet music and to learn the basics of technical areas that are in such demand today, namely, robotics, computer electronics and software. Our thoroughly modern player piano uses an electronic keyboard, solenoids to depress the keys, and for the brain of the system, a small but powerful computer which remembers the notes and activates the mini-robots at the correct time. Intermingled in the text, is an exploration of these basic mechanical devices as well as some theory for a useful learning experience. The main part of the book describes in detail the construction and operation of the player piano. You might think of this player piano project as a giant demonstration of interacting technologies needed to make music.

If this all sounds too technical, not to worry, ask any teenager with an iPhone and he/she will know the answer to most of your questions. I envision this project as something that a father/daughter or a high school team might tackle as a winter project. As I have in three other projects, I plan to provide all the needed information about the parts to buy and to give complete directions to build the project success-fully. I have already built one working model of the player piano and will build a second one using this book as my guide. This way, the circuits, the wiring and the software will be thoroughly checked out.

The computer used to replace the player piano rolls is an Arduino Mega, the "muscle car" of the Arduino family of computers. Arduino is renowned as THE tool for college students learning com-puter science. It is part of an open source system which means that all software is free and no patents or copyrights are involved. In addition, all available support systems such as the libraries and support groups are completely free. On my last visit to an electronics store, I saw at least 12 books written about the use of Arduino computers. The Mega computer used here costs less than $15. Only a basic laptop or PC is needed to download the Arduino software and upload the coded music to the control box of the player piano. All software needed to make beautiful music come to life is provided in the book or is available from Arduino, completely free.

This does not mean that the construction of the project is not challenging. Lots of parts must be ordered, and some, such as the solenoids, must be modified to reduce their noise level. Cabling and wiring the parts together is certainly a time-consuming activity. Coding the notes to play a song so that they can be interpreted properly by the computer is also a tedious process. Yet none of this is beyond the ability of a reasonably handy person working at the kitchen table. And with a little effort learning the software, you will be able to talk about programs like C++ and compilers with the best of them.

Chapter 1 which serves as an introduction and overview of the project, provides a summary of the capabilities and the specifications of the system. It also provides a guide to the main construction activities as well as a close estimate of the cost of the system and the amount of time needed to complete various activities.

The book is divided into 2 parts, each of which has 8 chapters:

Part 1: Provides all the instructions needed to build the player piano. It explores the musical symbols and describes the electronic circuits needed to activate the mini-robots and the keys.

Part 2: Describes the computer software needed to produce the music after it is uploaded to the Arduino Mega computer. The Arduino software (IDE) and the diagnostic software needed to resolve problems and make sure that the Robo sketch operates correctly are also described in Part 2.

Table of Contents

Part 1

Construction, Sheet Music and Electronics

Part 2

Arduino Computer and Software

LIST OF FIGURES

LIST OF PHOTOS

PART 1

CHAPTER 1

Introduction and Overview

First Steps

This project all began because of my son Steve and his interest in antique doorbell chimes. You're probably familiar with them, they play the "Westminster Chimes" notes on 4 tuned brass tubes about three feet long. Depending on the length of the tubes, they produce the notes F, A, G, C when they are tapped sharply at the top.

Steve owned a unit possibly 100 years old that was beyond salvation. The oil in the motor had congealed, the insulation was falling from the wires and the contacts of the distributor had burned out due to numerous short circuits. After some debate, (Steve was not one to give up easily when it came to preserving the originality of a precious antique) we decided to replace the guts of the chimes: the motor, the control unit and the solenoids that propel the plunger onto the tube. We picked an Arduino "Uno" the smallest computer of the Arduino family as the electronic brain to replace the motor and the distributor.

The Arduino family of computers is programmed using a derivative of the programming language called C. Simon Monk's excellent book for beginners "Programming Arduino" is perfect for those who might like to get more familiar with this subject but—have no fear, it is not necessary to do any programming in order to complete this project. Steve who like me worked at IBM for many years was an expert in C and C++ and did all the work for us.

The chime project was very successful and it still operates the chimes in his house to this day. This got me thinking that the keys of a piano could also be depressed by using solenoids as mini-robots under the control of a small computer. I was bored and between projects at the time and started researching the idea a couple of years ago.

Player Pianos/Keyboards

While researching player pianos, I soon discovered that my idea was far from unique. Piano manufacturers like Steinway and Yamaha already sell pianos with the player capability but the prices are steep. Steinway sells a kit that can be added to their $40,000 grand piano for an additional $20,000 to $30,000, while Yamaha sells a less expensive grand with the player piano feature for about $20,000.

Obviously, replacing the piano with a keyboard will result in a substantial saving but it has other benefits as well. These include: being light in weight, easy to move around and never having to be tuned. The volume is adjustable and it can even be played with earphones for completely quiet operation. And the new models also have a long list of built-in accompaniments such as a base or drums.

Although the keyboard's electronic imitation of the sound of the piano is very good and getting better, it will never match the sound of a hammer hitting a taut set of strings and therefore will never satisfy the purist. Nevertheless, keyboards are gradually being accepted and used more regularly. In a small church in Maine, a versatile musical director has a Yamaha keyboard just like mine. When he is not playing his guitar, he plays the keyboard alternating between piano and organ. Here in Naples, Florida, the church hall has a very good 88-key electronic piano, which makes beautiful music through a system of multiple speakers.

My Yamaha Keyboard

I started out with a visit to my local music store where I picked out a 76-key middle of the line Yamaha YPG-235. The special of the day included the stand and the "survival" kit which the salesman also threw in, bringing my purchase to a grand total of $268. The "survival" kit is a necessity. It includes the 120-volt power supply (this keyboard also operates on batteries), the earphones and the sustain pedal. Assuming that you assemble and wire the electronic parts yourself and that 50 of the 76 keys (much more on that subject later) are implemented, the cost of the rest of the project is about $380 for a total of $650.

As I mentioned in the preface, I envision this project as something that a father-daughter or a high school team might tackle as a winter project with the goal of building a modern, operational player piano. An important secondary goal is learning how to read sheet music and becoming familiar with basic technologies ranging from electronics to robots and computer software.

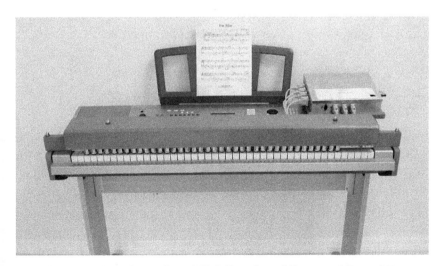

Photo 1.1 – Yamaha Keyboard With Soundproof Cover and Control Box

Photo 1.1 on page 3 shows the bottom of the solenoids (mini-robots) above the keyboard's keys (the cover is removed in Photo 2.4). The solenoids are connected with cables to the control box which houses the Arduino Mega and the electronics which drive the solenoids. On the right side of the control box, a cable can be connected to the USB port of any laptop or PC in order to upload the music to the Mega computer.

My intention is not just to describe how to build the control box but to explain the purpose of the components and how they work. The electronic board in the control box is shown in Photo 7.1. It looks very complicated at first sight. Upon closer inspection, however, you will see that there is only one unique Mosfet drive circuit with just four components, and that this exact drive circuit with four components is duplicated for each key. For the black keys, the electronic circuit going to the Mosfet drivers is slightly more complicated because the location of each black key is coded. I will be sure to explain how and why that is necessary when we get to it. Only two other circuits are needed—one for the volume control and one to activate the sustain capability of the keyboard. Of course, these circuits are already designed and checked out for you. Only the work of assembling and wiring them needs to be done.

The Author's Experience

I started working for IBM in 1956 at the very beginning of the computer era. At that time, computers had radio tubes and each bit of memory was a little core (like a bead) strung on four tiny wires. I have seen great changes in the last 60 years particularly in the enormous power of the microprocessors and their amazingly steep decrease in price. The Mega computer used here ($13) has more power than a room full of computer racks worth millions of dollars 60 years ago.

My interest in music started at a young age. My mother liked to brag about her precocious child (that would be me) by telling this story every chance she had. It seems that a group of her adult friends were discussing music and musical instruments. I was two or three years old at the time and only spoke French. When I was asked which instrument I would like to learn to play, I told them that I liked "la machine de Dame-Dame." Dame-Dame's machine was an old style wind-up Victrola! I was already interested in mechanical things at this tender age and, apparently, I recognized my lack of talent to play musical instruments.

Organization of the Book

The next chapter of Part One of the book is devoted to the process of constructing a player piano using the Yamaha keyboard. We will be able to mount a bar supporting the solenoids and modify the volume and sustain circuits without making any visible changes to the Yamaha keyboard as attested by Photo 1.1.

Next, we will learn all about musical symbols and how to read sheet music. Finally, we will explore the design of the electronic circuits which are used to drive the solenoids as well as two other circuits: the volume control and the sustain operation.

Part Two of the book is all about making the Arduino Mega computer play music. Why Arduino? The most important reason is that there is an appropriate computer model to do the job, namely, the Mega microprocessor with its large number of ports. The popularity of the Arduino family of computers, their high quality and their low price were added bonuses.

The hardware section describes how to connect the electronic circuits designed in Part One to the Mega. We will see that the wiring consists of plugging 53 wires in 53 of the 54 output ports and connecting a few low voltage wires from the appropriate outputs of the computer to the solenoid drivers. The USB cable is the only connection needed from the Mega to the PC.

Then we get immersed in software. Several chapters are devoted to the player piano sketches (in the world of Arduino, the software programs are called sketches). The purpose of this software is to transform the sheet music information so that the keyboard will play the correct notes and sounds. This software, named "Robo" and written by Steve is highly efficient. A minute's worth of musical notes (about 200 notes) requires about 3000 bytes out of the 258,048 bytes of the available memory in the Mega. Therefore, more than 90 minutes worth of music can be played with one upload to the Mega.

The next chapters in Part Two, describe how the notes are coded so that they can be interpreted by the Robo sketch. Each coded note has eight features which describe the note (such as its beat or whether it is part of a chord). Considering the amount of repetition there is in music, the coding may be tedious but it is not difficult.

And, finally, we describe diagnostic programs which can be used to play the scales by activating one key at a time to check out the operation of the solenoids or to troubleshoot a problem.

The Challenges

For me, making sense out of the little ovals with tails sitting on or between the 10 lines of the sheet music turned out to be my biggest challenge during this project. Learning anything new is, of course, always a challenge.

When selecting the electronic parts, the main challenge is to find a push type solenoid with the right form factor (it has to fit in less space than the width of a key) yet it has to be powerful enough to depress the key. The plunger travel has to move at least 3/8 of an inch to depress a key fully. In addition, because we need so many solenoids, they have to be inexpensive. The ones that I selected meet the specifications but they are too noisy for this application and need to be modified. I would have been happier with a higher-quality solenoid but I could not find one at a good price.

Another challenge is to make the music sound less robotic (even though the mini-robots create it). The volume control and the sustain action help a lot but more work could be done to make the music sound as if it is produced by a true musician.

The main challenge writing the player piano sketch "Robo" is coding the chords (when several keys are depressed at the same time). Especially difficult is Beethoven's version of chords where some of the notes are modified during the time that the chord is being played. I can vouch for the fact that the mini-robots are up to task but I can't even imagine how an accomplished pianist performs such a feat!

Due to the large number of keys, wiring the control box so that it does not look like a rat's nest turned out to be a challenge. It is important to use as large a breadboard as possible. Using small wire and making neat solder joints also helps.

In the construction of the bar that holds the solenoids, the location of the mounting hole for the solenoids is critical (otherwise the solenoid plungers will not line up with the middle of the keys). Vertically, the solenoids have to line up perfectly so that they all have a minimum of 3/8 inches of travel. To solve this problem, I made a simple jig which worked out very well.

Beyond these difficulties, the project is very straight forward. With a lot of time and a good deal of patience, it can be completed by any competent do-it yourselfer.

Summary of Chapter 1

To review the main points described in this chapter:

- The construction instructions shown in this book are for a YamahaYPG-235 Keyboard. There are no changes to the keyboard that would detract from the instrument's value. Similar keyboards can also be used.

- The computer which controls the operation of the keys is an Arduino Mega. All Arduino software is free and open source. Using another computer is not recommended.

- Up to 76 solenoids (45 white keys and 31 black keys) can be mounted on two horizontal bars to activate the keys.

- As shown in the photo, the solenoids are cabled to the control box which houses the Arduino Mega computer and the solenoid drivers.

- Each of the Mega computer's ports is wired to a simple four component Mosfet driver (the circuit diagram and the wiring charts are provided).

- The Arduino sketch "Robo" which interprets the notes and activates the solenoids is provided.

- The code to transcribe the beat of the music and the musical notes from the sheet music to the Arduino Mega is created on a PC which is attached to the Mega with the USB cable. Once the music has been coded and verified it can be uploaded to the Mega and played as often as desired.

- Musical arrangements with different beats or added pauses can be coded to re-arrange the sheet music or to create entirely new music and tunes.

A great deal of satisfaction and pleasure can be derived from the learning experience of building this player piano. It is capable of playing any of your favorite songs as well as music that you create yourself. In addition, building this project provides an invaluable learning experience in some of todays most desirable and in demand high-tech areas.

CHAPTER 2

Building the Player Piano

Selecting a Keyboard

There is a lot to consider when it comes to selecting an electronic keyboard. The most important qualities to look at are the sound of the instrument, the feel of the keys, the accompaniments that are provided and the price. Luckily, I was just looking to convert a keyboard into a player piano so I could ignore the subjective factors and focus on the price and the features, and ultimately came up with the Yamaha YPG-235. Including the stand and the accessories which are sold as a kit called the "Survival Kit" (120-volt power supply, earphones and sustain pedal—all required) the price was $268.

Because the Arduino Mega has a maximum of 54 output ports, there is a limit of 76 keys that can be activated by the Mega. If you can manage with fewer keys, it's possible to significantly reduce the complexity and cost by selecting a 50-key keyboard or a 61-key keyboard of which only 50 keys are activated. The decoder for the black keys could be eliminated because the Mega's 54 ports would then be sufficient to operate all the active keys. My second choice would have been a 61-key keyboard of which there is also a great deal of choice. This subject will be re-examined in Chapter 5.

It's possible to use the directions from this book on other keyboards with more or fewer keys or even a real piano. Should you attempt that, the solenoid bar would obviously have to be mounted differently for the various instruments and the sound absorbing cover would have to be modified.

Mounting the Solenoids

In this chapter we describe the way the solenoid are mounted on an aluminum bar which in turn is mounted on a wooden crossbar on the keyboard. The solenoids (and we will devote the next chapter to their selection and their need to be modified) are JF-0730B's which are manufactured by various Chinese companies. They are 12-volt DC devices drawing 1 amp. The plunger travel distance, which is critical, is 10mm (a little more than 3/8 inches). The body of the solenoid is a little more than ½ inch wide, ¾ inch deep and 1.25 inches high. Since the keys on a keyboard are a little more than 7/8 inch wide, there is plenty of room to accommodate 11 solenoids in the 10 inches spanned by 11 keys.

The solenoids are mounted on an 1.5 inch aluminum flat bar, 1/8 inch thick, cut down to 41.25 inches from 48 inches. Aluminum bars like these can be bought at Home Depot for about $11 each. Two are needed, one for the white keys and one for the black keys. The 7 inches left-over from each bar will be used to build a testing device for 5 solenoids.

The back of the solenoids have two threaded holes which accommodate M3 metric screws 6mm long. In an effort to keep the solenoid noise to a minimum, we will mount the bars with rubber grommets around the mounting screws. We don't want the aluminum bar to touch the wooden crossbar, so the solenoid mounting screws must have flat heads to remain flush with the aluminum bar. The screws need to be short so that they will not dig into the insulation around the solenoids' coil. To accomplish all of this, the ideal screws are steel, flat head screws, metric size M3, 6mm long. In quantities of 100 they cost about $6.

Home Depot does not carry a good selection of small metric nuts, bolts and screws—the selection at Ace Hardware is much better.

When a large quantity of screws like these is needed, plan ahead and order them from Grainger's. In quantities of 100, the cost is generally one quarter or less than the retail price. I don't have much luck finding or ordering screws online from Ace or Grainger but they are happy to special order them for you from the store. They can be found more easily at online specialists like BoltDepot.com.

Mounting the Solenoids

As I have mentioned, the installation of the solenoids on the aluminum bar is critical. We will see that part of the 10mm of plunger travel will be used to quiet the solenoids. It is therefore critical that all solenoids line up in a straight line so that they just touch the keyboard keys when they are de-energized. We have seen that the solenoids are attached with flat head screws, which means that the holes in the aluminum bar will be countersunk so that the heads do not protrude beyond the bar. This, in turn, means that there is no wiggle room to correct any misalignment of the solenoid.

To assure that the mounting holes are drilled uniformly in the aluminum bar, we will first build the simple jig that is pictured below (Photo 2.1). To make sure that the jig performs its alignment properly, check it out according to the following directions. Press the jig tightly and clamp it to the bottom of a left-over piece of aluminum bar. Drill the pilot holes, then the 1/8 inch mounting holes, then countersink them and make sure that several solenoids can be mounted correctly. In case you countersink too deeply, grind one millimeter or so from the mounting screw so that it won't dig into the insulation of the coil.

Photo 2.1 – Solenoid Mounting Jig

The Jig

The jig shown above was made from a kitchen cabinet hinge that I found in my junk box. Ignore the three large holes. Three things are important. One, the bottom of the jig must have a 90 degree bend about 1/8 inches wide. Two, the two small, 1/16 inch pilot holes (7/64 can be used as well) need to match the mounting holes of the solenoid exactly. Three, a center line indicating the middle of the mounting holes must be marked at the top of the jig so that the jig can be lined up with the middle of the keys.

The next step is to mark on the aluminum bar with a sharp pencil where the middle of each key is located. Don't expect to measure the space between two keys accurately enough to transfer this measurement to the bar. Even a minute error will grow to an unacceptable error when multiplied 45 times. Instead, place the bar in front of the keys and mark each space between keys. Then, divide by two and mark the center line. Double-check your work with a pair of dividers or calipers to make sure that the distance between center lines is uniform.

At this point, align the center lines drawn on the bar with the center mark on the jig, then press the 90 degree bend of the jig firmly against the bottom of the bar and clamp it in place with vise grip pliers. If at all possible, drill the pilot holes and the 1/8 inch mounting holes on a drill-press. If a drill-press is not available, clamp the bar vertically in your vise, then, using the level in your hand-drill, drill the holes as square and true as possible. Do not keep the drill bit in the pilot holes of the jig any longer that necessary—we don't want the pilot holes to become oval or enlarged.

We have quite a bit of work to do to prepare the solenoids before they can be installed on the bar, so let's describe how the aluminum bars are attached to the keyboard first.

Mounting the Aluminum Bars on the Keyboard

These instructions apply to a Yamaha YPG-235 but can easily be modified for a different keyboard. The basic idea is to mount a straight 2 inch by ¾ inch wooden crossbar securely on the keyboard about ¼ inch above the keys and ¼ inch away from the front of the black keys. It will become the base for the two aluminum bars on which the solenoids are mounted. In the case of the Yamaha, it can be done without drilling any new holes in the keyboard. This may not be the case with other keyboards.

Finding a straight board (straight means not bowed and not twisted) is not always easy, but since this one is only 48.25 inches long, a clear section can be cut from a 6 foot board 4 or 6 inches wide. #2 pine is fine as long as the section selected does not have any knots. Take advantage of Home Depot's policy to allow customers to select the best piece of wood for their job.

The 2 inch wooden crossbar is mounted on a small support bracket at each end. These support brackets are in turn attached to the keyboard with the existing mounting hardware for the stand. Photo 2.3, below, shows a picture of the left support bracket. (The right support bracket is a mirror image of the left). It also shows the 2 inch crossbar and the aluminum mounting bar for the solenoids.

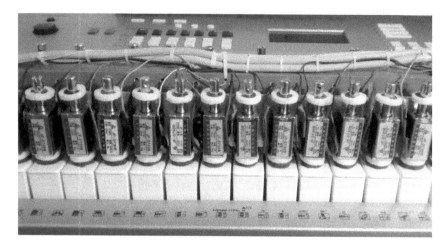

Photo 2.2 – Crossbar with Solenoids Mounted

The crossbar in Photo 2.2 is obscured by the 12 solenoids but in the middle, one can see an 1/8 inch hole in the crossbar that is used to tie down the cables and through which passes one of the four gray wires which supply the power to the +12-volt bus from the control box (the +12-volt, #14 copper bus wire is not visible). At each solenoid position, there is another 1/8 inch hole in the crossbar through which one of the solenoid wires passes and is attached to this +12-volt bus. The second solenoid wire is connected to the cable that goes to the control box connector and from there connects to the middle pin of the appropriate Mosfet driver. Lace the two solenoid wires together if they interfere with the plunger operation.

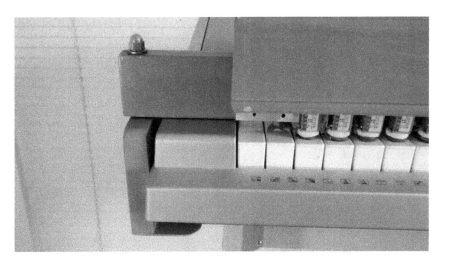

Photo 2.3 – The Left Support Bracket

The support brackets are 4 inches wide and 3 and 5/8 inches high. They are made from ¾ inch pine stock. The bottom metal plate, made of 1/16 inch steel stock, is 4 by 2 and 3/8 inches in size. The plate is attached to the pine bracket with three #8 flat head wood screws ¾ inches long. A ¼ inch hole, 5/8 inch and 3/8 inch from the corner of the plate is used to attach the plate to the leg stand mounting screw. A ½ inch semicircle cut-out is needed to clear the foot of the keyboard. Finally, a 6.5 inch threaded rod (1/4 inch in diameter with 20 threads per inch) is used to attach the wooden crossbar to the two support brackets with acorn nuts.

Mounting the Control Box

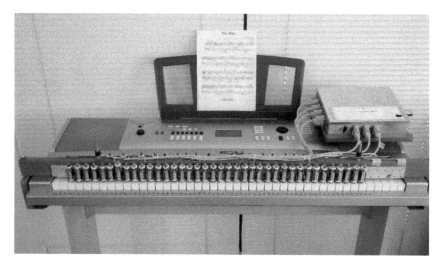

Photo 2.4 – Player Piano without Cover

Above and below we find photos showing the keyboard with the attached solenoid bars, and a close-up showing the control box and the cables that connect it to the solenoids.

Note that the cables are laced together (with waxed nylon lacing cord) for a professional looking job. 1/8 inch holes are drilled every few inches near the top of the wooden cross-bar to attach the cables to the wooden bar.

The aluminum control box is a standard size measuring 10 by 8 inches, 2 inches tall. It's a tight fit to house the connectors, the Arduino Mega and the drive circuits so anything smaller will not work.

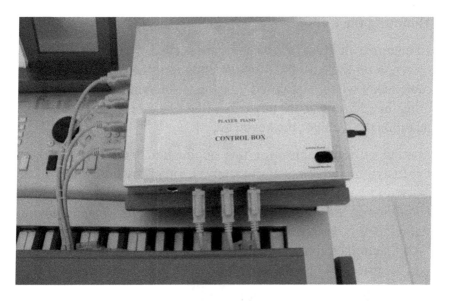

Photo 2.5 – Control Box and Cable Connectors

Under the control box (only visible in the front of the picture) is a simple 10 by 11 inch shelf made from ¼ inch plywood. It is mounted 2 inches above the speaker at the same angle as the top of the keyboard. Its support, which is anchored to the back of the keyboard, is also made of ¼ inch plywood. 4 sheet metal screws fasten the plywood to the body of the keyboard. The keyboard plastic is thin at this location, so don't over-tighten the mounting screws.

A better location might be on a folding shelf attached to the right-hand leg of the stand, where it would not block the speaker or some of the controls. The cables would be a little longer and accessibility to the controls in the control box would be hampered somewhat but it could be a good trade off. If I were to do it again I would choose the leg location. Your choice.

Mounting the Cables

To energize all 76 keys, 10 cables are needed. 10 cable sockets are shown, 6 on the side and 4 on the bottom of the control box. Each cable has 9 wires, 8 are used to activate solenoids and 1 is used to bring the +12 volts to the power bus (the #14 bare copper conductor) that runs the width of the keyboard.

Making custom cables for this application would be quite an expensive undertaking. Fortunately, I found the equivalent of an extension cord with a male connector on one end and a female connector on the other end. It is 6 feet long and has 9 colored wires with DB-9 connectors at each end. It can be bought online at "All Electronics.com" in California. The catalog number is CB-397 and the price is $4 per cable.

Because the cables are 6 feet long, there is a substantial amount of cable left over after they are connected to the control box which is, on average, about three feet away. The other half of the cable is usable as long as the connector on the control box is of the opposite gender. I found that 6 of these cables are sufficient. The DB-9 connectors to be mounted on the left side and bottom of the box can also be ordered from All Electronics. Order 7 of one type and 5 of the other, that way you will have two left over to make test cables to check the solenoids after they are installed and wired to their respective cables. The DB-9 connectors cost less than 50 cents each at All Electronics.

While working on the solenoid noise problem, I thought that a good sound proof cover would greatly alleviate the problem. To that end I built an oak cover, thinking that the heavy wood would reduce the transmission of sound and I drilled hundreds of holes in the wood to absorb the unwanted noise as is done in sound absorbing ceiling tiles. The resulting tests showed a reduction of 2 to 3 DB's in the amount of noise generated by the solenoids.

The Solenoid Cover

Despite helping with the noise problem, I did not like the looks of this massive cover, so I tried other ideas. I settled on 4½ inch chair railing sold at Home Depot. It is a simple molding with a small groove on top and bottom and rounded edges. I looked for a part number online but could not find it among the hundreds of designs available. This simple design allows you to rip the board in the middle to provide two 2¼ inch wide pieces for the sides of the cover. The noise tests also indicated a reduction of about 2 DB but seeing that the wood is only 3/8 inch thick, I opted not to drill holes. Possibly 1/16 inch stick-on foam strips would have the same sound reducing effect.

Photo 2.6 – Inside View of the Cover

Above is a photo of the inside of the cover (Photo 1.1 shows the outside of the cover). It shows the cutout for the cables and the mounting plate that fits on the two 5/16 studs which are inserted in the 2 inch crossbar. One 5/16 inch grommet fits in each mounting plate and two more fit inside each of the 9/16 inch holes in the top of the cover. This way the cover is insulated with sound absorbing rubber in all directions.

Mounting the Electronics in the Control Box

In addition to the ten DB-9 connectors, two circuit boards (4.5 by 6.25 inch from Radio Shack) are needed to mount the Mosfet drive circuits (one for each key). In my case, there are 60 drivers but the design accommodates 76 driver circuits. The 2 by 4 inch circuit board of the Arduino Mega computer is also mounted in the box. The picture below shows the general location of these components.

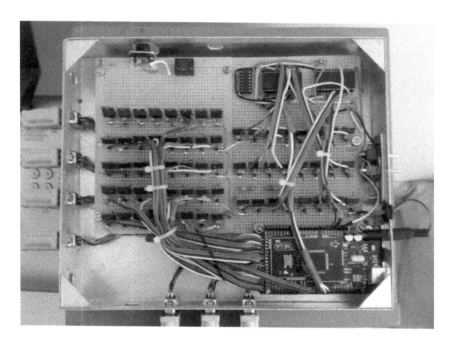

Photo 2.7 – View of the Open Control Box

Notice that the Arduino is in the right, bottom corner of the box. This is necessary because the USB cable for the PC connection and the 12-volt power cable are both plugged into the right side of the Arduino board. To provide more room for the other boards, the

Arduino can be mounted above the circuit boards. Two 3/8 inch stand-offs are used. The stand-offs are just hollow ¼ inch nylon plastic tubes through which a ¾ inch long 4/40 screw is threaded. The bottom of the screw is locked to the breadboard with a 4/40 nut. Use a fiber washer under the top nut to avoid scratching the Arduino board or causing a short circuit. Notice also, on the right, the small plate on which the on/off switch and the master reset switch are mounted. Photo 7.1 of the open control box is annotated to describe the components in greater detail.

Breadboards

Solderable breadboards to mount the components come in a variety of sizes and configurations, but they can be pricey. The one with the most real estate that will fit in the control box is the Radio Shack model with 2200 holes and that costs about $5. It measures about 4.5 by 6.25 inches, two of them are needed. They are bolted together and can be mounted on three ½ inch standoffs to the bottom of the control box. Stick four felt feet on the bottom of the box to keep the screw heads from damaging the surface on which the control box will rest.

Printed Circuit Boards

It is only because we are building one player piano at a time that we are using breadboards to mount the electronic components. Normally, once the circuits are checked out, a printed circuit board (PC board) is designed and built. Designing a circuit board of the size needed here is a serious undertaking. But with the "Pad2Pad" CAD/CAM (Computer Aided Design/Computer Aided Manufacturing) program it can be done even by a novice like me.

Photo 2.8 below shows the results of my effort. It looks great and it has impressive statistics: 3584 traces (equivalent to wires), 2720 pads (like the round circles on the breadboards), 1062 holes, 298 vias (the through connections going from the top side of the board to the bottom side).

But, the statistics don't show one problem: it has 9 errors. The errors can easily be corrected but I have learned a lot since this first attempt: if I were to try it again, I would design an Arduino shield which would reduce the wiring to an even greater extent. The cost of PC boards is highly dependent on quantity. For example, one unit like mine (6 by 8 inches) costs $175 but 50 units cost $577 or about $11 per unit. Considering that the quality of the PC board is far better than that of the breadboard and that so much wiring could be avoided, it certainly would be worth, say, $20. If there appears to be a demand for it, I will design an Arduino shield that plugs into the Mega and provides drivers for 25 solenoids (2 or 3 shields would be needed). But for now, we will have to live with the breadboards.

Photo 2.8 – Home-designed PC Board

Summary

This chapter described the three items that are mounted on a keyboard to turn it into a player piano. They consist of the aluminum bars on which the solenoids are mounted, the 2 inch wooden crossbar supporting the aluminum bars and the brackets that support the wooden crossbar. The control box and its support bracket are also described. The pictures and dimensions are for a 76-key Yamaha YGP-235, but we have seen that different keyboards can also be turned into player pianos.

Mounting the components in the control box has also been described briefly. They consist of the Arduino computer, two breadboard circuits and, depending on the configuration to be selected, 7 to 10 cable connectors.

With these jobs completed, we can now tackle the difficult task of selecting and modifying our min-robot solenoids in the next chapter.

CHAPTER 3

The Solenoid Mini-Robots

Selecting the Solenoid

Selecting the best solenoid for this application is not an easy task. Solenoids come in all sizes. The smallest that I have worked with pushed a single wire in a dot matrix printer. At the other extreme, electromagnets can be incredibly strong. In junkyards, cars are actually lifted with them. Online, you can find excellent descriptions of the solenoids' operation and images of hundreds types and styles.

Because we need so many of them, we need a good quality device that is also inexpensive. The important specifications are as follows:

A "push" type (as opposed to the more common "pull" type)

Approximately size: ¾ x ¾ by 1.5 inches long.

12 volt operation if possible. 1 amp or less for the current

$3 or less for the price.

I ordered and checked out a dozen solenoids that were close to the specifications shown above. Of these, I selected the best five. I spent a lot of time testing the high quality Ledex, but finally concluded that its power was too low and that it would be too difficult to attach a foot to the end of the plunger shaft. The curves below show the power of these five solenoids depending on the amount of electrical power, in watts, that is applied to them.

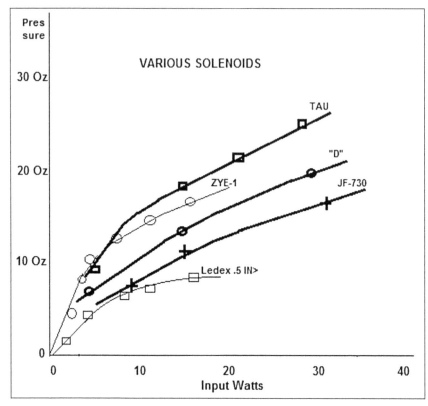

Figure 3.1 – Power of Various Solenoids

The x-axis shows the electrical power in watts. One watt is equal to one amp multiplied by one volt. So if at 12 volts our test solenoid (type JF) draws one amp we find that it uses 12 watts and develops 9 oz. of force. Since depressing a piano key only requires 4 oz, we are comfortably in the operating zone.

This is a good time to explore the very basis of electrical circuits, Ohm's law. The well-known analogy for an electrical circuit is the water pipe where the pressure of the water is equivalent to the voltage and the amount of water flow is the current measured in amperes or amps. The size of the pipe which restricts the amount of water that can flow through the pipe is analogous to the resistance in ohms in an electrical circuit.

Ohm's law simply states that V (volts) divided by I (the current in amps) equals R (the resistance in ohms). In the case of the solenoid, it has hundreds of turns of fine wire to produce the magnetic force that drives the plunger. All this fine wire has a certain amount of resistance. In the case of the JF-0730, if you were to measure the resistance of the coil with the ohmmeter section of a multi-meter, you would find that it is 17 ohms. Applying Ohms law and solving for I (amps) we find that at 12 volts, the current is .7 amps (even though the label on the solenoid says "1 A").

The water analogy also applies to the power of the solenoid. Imagine a waterfall with a turbine at the bottom which generates electricity. It is obvious that, if the waterfall were twice as high (V x 2) or if the amount of water were twice as great (I x 2), the power would double in each case. The same thing would happen with the solenoid if the voltage were doubled. Unfortunately, the solenoid would quickly overheat and burn up. The short operating time of the solenoids in this application would allow us to increase the voltage substantially without damage but I chose to stay within the specifications.

The tests revealed that there were two possible problem areas. First, although the label on the solenoid says "1 amp," the actual current at 12 volts DC is only .7 amps which reduces the electrical power to 8.4 watts. According to the curves, this reduces the strength to depress the keys to about 8 oz. Fortunately, we are still well into the operating zone.

The other potential problem has to do with the way we energize the solenoid. When we play a full note, the key will stay energized for 2 seconds (when the beat of the song is 120 beats per minute). But when we play a 1/16th note, the solenoid will only stay energized for 125 milliseconds (1/8 second). I checked to make sure that the short pulses and the lower than expected power would still allow the solenoid to activate the keys correctly and it does. Much more will be said about length of notes and how to activate them with our mini-robots later in the book. Ohm's law will also be revisited when we adjust the volume of the speakers under computer control.

JF-0730 Solenoid Noise Problem

What do I consider too noisy and what is acceptable? I think that we should strive to keep the noise level equivalent to the amount of noise created by the keys hitting bottom when they are played by hand. Just listening to the amount of noise that they make would be too subjective; we need a better way of measuring sound levels. Fortunately, the smart phone comes to the rescue with a sound measuring app. Although decibels (DB's) are also used to express ratios, here they will be used only to measure sound levels. Because DB's are measured on a logarithmic scale, the results are different from what we are accustomed to. For example, if sound B is twice as loud as sound A it would be 3 DB greater not twice the number of DB's. If sound B measures 40 DB and sound A measures 20 DB (an increase of 20 DB) B would actually be 100 times louder.

DB measurements vary greatly depending on the distance that the measuring device is from the source of the sound. The DB measurements that we make in our tests are always taken with the smart phone three feet away from the source of the sound which in most cases is a solenoid or the speaker from the Yamaha keyboard. Needless to say, the ambient sound in the room will affect the readings. One time, I seemed to get readings somewhat higher than previous readings under the same conditions. It was raining hard that day and the added noise of the rain hitting the roof of the house raised the ambient noise considerably. To get good readings do your work in quiet surroundings.

Noise reduction Techniques

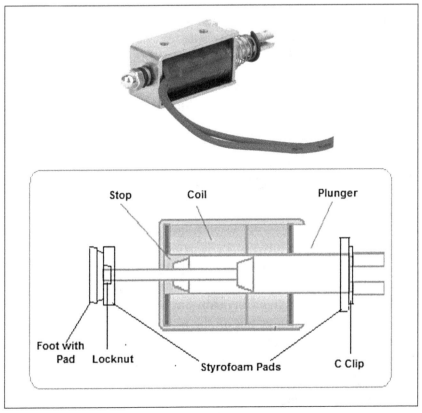

Figure 3.2 – Image and Cross-section of the JF-0730 Solenoid

Having settled on the JF-0730 as the best compromise as far as quality, size, power and price, the next step was to try various methods of reducing the excessive noise that the solenoid made when driving the keys. It's worth mentioning that all the solenoids tested were too noisy and would have required modifications. Quiet solenoids do exist but they cost at least 5 times as much as the JF-0730. The figure above shows the image of the solenoid, the operation of this simple device and the source of the noise.

It should be noted that the noise is greatly amplified when the sole-noid is mounted on a solid surface. When you activate a solenoid held in your hand there is little noise. On the other hand, the noise becomes unacceptable when the solenoid is mounted firmly on a solid surface. We will therefore work on the mounting as well as on the solenoid itself.

There are three sources of unwanted noise but the main one is caused by the seating of the plunger when it slams against its stop. As the diagram above shows the plunger cone comes to rest in a V shaped part of the body of the solenoid. The main trade-off here is to reduce the noise without reducing the travel of the plunger any more than is absolutely necessary.

I tried a variety of possible solutions including machining a grove in the cone and fitting a tiny rubber "o" ring in the grove. Nothing that I tried worked as well as simply stopping the plunger from hitting the cone at all. That can be done easily by fitting a Styrofoam pad on the body of the plunger beneath the "C" clip. The fit should be tight so that the pad stays put on the plunger shaft. It should not be more than 1/8 inch thick nor anymore than 5/8 inch in diameter. I tried a number of other materials such as soft rubber, cork, foam, plastic, felt, balsa wood and Styrofoam earplugs. Because they are so easy to make, ¼ inch diameter rubber grommets that are sliced in two would be my second choice. I discovered the ear plugs too late to use them but they seemed very promising.

The simplest way to make these pads (to my knowledge, they cannot be bought) is to buy rigid ¾ inch thick closed cell insulation. Drill a 3/16 inch hole in the edge of the Styrofoam, and then cut 1/8 inch thick slices. The slices will further be cut in 5/8 inch squares and trimmed to round them off. They need to be rounded so that the corners don't interfere with the next solenoid when the plungers rotate during their operation.

The second source of unwanted noise occurs when the foot of the shaft is pushed back to its rest position by the key after it has performed its task of playing a note (we will describe a foot for the shaft shortly). Here again, after trying a variety of materials, I could not find anything that worked better than a Styrofoam pad. In this case, the pad can be sliced thinner than 1/8 inch. It only needs to be slightly thicker than the brass lock-nut that holds the foot in place. With a 7/32 hole, the Styrofoam will fit over the nut. It can be glued to the foot so that it will not ride up and down on the shaft.

The third unwanted noise occurs when the end of the plunger shaft hits the keyboard key. We will describe a foot that reduces this noise in the next section.

A Jig to Slice the Styrofoam Pads

The picture below shows a miter box-like jig to slice Styrofoam or other materiel such as cork, rubber or balsa wood. This mini-miter box has a nice feature to determine the thickness of the washer-like wafer being cut. The material to be cut presses against an adjustable stop while it is sliced with a razor blade. This simple stop is a quarter inch locking nut that is adjusted in and out of the wood block at the end of the miter box groove. The best cutting devices are a serrated knife or a razor blade. My experience is that the razor blade works better.

While in the hospital, I discovered that inexpensive ear plugs are about the right consistency to make good sound absorbing washers. Being round cylinders about ½ inch in diameter they only need to be drilled and sliced. To drill them, use a very high speed drill bit slightly larger in diameter than the finished result. One of these ear plugs was sliced for Photo 3.1. The ear plugs can be obtained from Amazon.

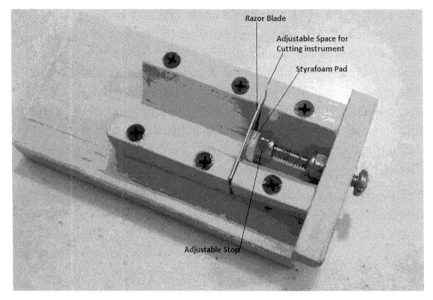

Photo 3.1 – Image of the Miter Box Slicing Jig

The Solenoid Foot

The foot is an important part of the mini-robot solenoid design because it has to depress the keys reliably and quietly. The round metal acorn nut provided with the solenoid does not work for two reasons; one, over time it will damage the plastic top of the keys and two, it is very noisy. One might think that since the plunger already rests on the key no additional noise would be produced when it depresses the key farther but that is not the case. Once again a smart phone app—one allowing videos to be played in slow motion—was used to resolve the mystery.

What actually happens is that the plunger bounces when the key hits bottom. It is at that time that the noise is created. I first thought that a plastic or rubber cap could be fitted on the end of the plunger shaft to absorb the pressure, but that did not work well. The solutions described below are effective, but they are time consuming to build.

Both solutions involve screwing a foot on the shaft of the plunger. A brass nut must be purchased to replace the acorn nut furnished with the solenoid. The nut size is M-3, part # HN4B00300-100P1 at Grainger Industrial Supply (about $6 for 100).

Photo 3.2 below shows two different feet that can be attached to the solenoid shaft. On the left, the nut is glued to the flat part of a 5/8 inch button (#570000022 at Jo Ann's fabric; $1 for 20 buttons). Super glue works well but J-B Weld's two-part epoxy (3960 PSI) is stronger. It does have a 24 hour cure time so it must remain undisturbed for that length of time. Be sure to sand off the glaze from the brass nuts and the buttons with medium sandpaper for a good bond. Apply some of the glue to the sides of the nut for maximum strength. Screw the nut on the shaft (3 turns) to keep the glue from filling the hole. Make sure that the shaft is at a 90 degree angle to the button while the glue dries.

As shown on the right, the brass nut is attached to a small round brass plate (the size of a dime) by soldering it on. I used some thick brass gasket material to make the small round plate but I realize that it is not easily available in small quantities. An automobile parts store may be able to help.

Photo 3.2 – Image of the Button Foot and the Soldered Foot

Before soldering the parts together, tin them by applying a thin layer of solder on the plate and to the nut after both have been sanded. Add a very small amount of solder when soldering the parts together at a 90 degree angle. Attach the nut to the shaft (3 turns) for ease of handling and to make sure that the solder does not fill the threads of the nut. The solder joint is easy to redo if the location or the angle is not right. It does take practice to do a good job. By all means, use the epoxy if you have problems with the soldering.

Two more jobs need to be done to the foot to make it operate quietly. For the bottom of the foot, I got the best results from 1/16 inch stick-on foam which I bought at Home Depot. Stick-on felt works also, but I found it to be a little noisier. A 1/16 inch thick pad similar to the one below the C clip will prevent the nut from hitting the body of the solenoid when the key pushes the shaft back up after the key is released. I have not tried the sliced earplugs at this location but I expect that they would work very well.

Measuring the Noise from the Keys

Measuring the amount of noise caused by the keys with the smart phone app is much easier when a diagnostic sketch which operates the keys one at a time is running in the Mega. Until we get to that point, the best solution is to generate 12 volts DC with eight 1.5-volt "D" batteries wired in series. After the solenoids have been installed, they can be checked out with the 12-volt battery supply. To add some versatility to the testing, build the "D" battery supply with taps so that voltages from 6 volts to 12 volts can easily be selected. Be advised that soldering wires to "D" batteries with a 25-watt soldering iron is difficult. The area has to be sanded clean and additional flux from what is in the soldering wire is needed. Make sure that the solder really melts into the battery material.

First, bundle four "D" batteries together and tape them in one bundle of four with duct tape. Wire them in series by soldering a wire (about 22-guage, stranded) from the negative of one battery to the positive of the next battery. When finished, you should have a negative wire and +6 volts on the positive wire of the fourth battery. At this point, wire another group of four batteries using short pieces of bare wire between batteries so that a clip jumper can easily be attached to the bare wire. You will end up with another bundle of four batteries. When the negative terminal is connected to the positive of the first group of batteries, voltages of 7.5, 9, 10.5 and 12 volts will be generated. Using clip jumpers any one of these voltages can easily be selected.

Until the diagnostic programs can be run, we will do our testing (noise and continuity tests of the cables) with the batteries. With the lower voltages (7.5, 9.0 and 10.5 volts), we will be able to perform "marginal" testing on the solenoids to make sure that they all operate at the same lower voltage. If they all work equally well at, say, 7.5 volts, it's an acceptable result even if a few solenoids operate at 6 volts. That will tell us that they were installed and work correctly. The solenoids need to press down on the keys with equal force for the musical sounds to have the same volume.

With the solenoids mounted as discussed above and modified for noise reduction, here are some representative noise measurements obtained in the tests using the 12-volt battery to activate the solenoids.

- Yamaha off, noise of the keys hitting bottom when pushed down by hand: approximately 23 DB
- Yamaha off, noise of depressing the keys with the modified JF-0730 solenoid: average of many tests 25 DB
- Yamaha off, best results using a better solenoid (Ledex): average of many tests 22 DB.

Testing the Solenoids

After all the solenoids are modified, it is time to test them. We want to make sure that the solenoids work correctly and that they operate quietly. I suggest two tests using our battery with multiple voltages and our DB meter. The DB measurements will indicate how successful the noise reduction was. The marginal test which is performed with the lower battery taps tells us that the solenoid power is adequate.

We will test five solenoids at a time. Using a left-over piece of aluminum bar about 7 inches long, drill the ten mounting holes for five solenoids with the jig as before. Also drill and countersink two mounting holes with grommets for the aluminum bar and mount it near the middle of the wooden crossbar. Mount the short aluminum bar so that the middle test solenoid activates the note middle C. (Should this test need to be repeated, we want to be able to duplicate the set-up).

Label each solenoid to be tested from 1 to 76 and keep a written record of the results. For the noise test place the DB meter 3 feet away from the key middle C and turn off the keyboard.

Twist one lead from each of the five test solenoids together with a wire nut and with a jumper connect it to the ground (-) of the battery. Clip another jumper wire to the other solenoid lead, one solenoid at a time and operate it by touching the battery taps at 12 volts, 10.5 volts, 9 volts and 7.5 volts. If everything was done correctly, including the mounting and the noise suppression, you should get consistent results both in noise readings and minimum voltage operation for each of the five solenoids. You may want to rotate the plunger of the solenoid under test to make sure that it operates at the low voltage in all positions. I have had slightly bent plungers that stick in some positions as they rotate when they are activated.

For the noise test, it is just a matter of averaging several readings at the 12-volt operating voltage. If a solenoid is clearly too loud, this is the time to correct the problem. Check the space between the C ring and the body of the solenoid. I have had some solenoids where this space is greater than average and it required a slightly thicker pad. Record all your results!

When you are satisfied with the results of the solenoid testing in groups of five, these solenoids can be un-wired and installed on the long aluminum bars for the white and black keys. Install your most problematic solenoids on the end of the bar where they are used the least amount of time.

Summary of Chapter 3

In this chapter, the selection process for the JF-0730 solenoid was described and compared to other candidate solenoids. The operation of solenoids was explained as well as the need to modify them to reduce the noise that they produce.

Ohm's law was discussed and applied to the operation of the solenoids. Techniques to reduce the noise that originates in three locations in the solenoid were explored. Different ways to build the foot of the solenoid plunger were discussed.

Using a 12-volt battery pack, tests were proposed to actuate the solenoids at lower voltage (marginal tests) and also to obtain noise readings for one-to-one comparisons between solenoids. The solenoids that are out of the average range need to be reworked before installing them on the aluminum bars.

CHAPTER 4

Sheet Music, Musical Symbols

Background

Computers are really dumb. Every minor detail has to be explained to them and they only know 1's and 0's. To make up for this, they are lightning fast—in the half second that it takes to play a quarter-note, the Aduino Mega performs 8 million operations. We don't have to be concerned that it will be overworked: between bursts of activity it idles most of the time.

To make our computer activate the mini-robots, we will write a sketch (programs are called sketches in Arduino-speak), named "Robo" to tell the Mega what to do with the information that we provide about the notes. This note information is provided consecutively for each note as it is found in the sheet music for a song.

There are eight bits of information provided for each note to determine characteristics like: what the note's pitch is, how long it lasts and which mini-robot should be activated. Fortunately, music contains a great deal of repetition so that the line of type containing this information can often be repeated or modified slightly with the edit function of the Arduino IDE software instead of requiring a full line of typing.

The job of the Robo sketch (which is up-loaded from the PC to the Mega computer once per music session) is to interpret the eight bits of information concerning the note, activate the solenoid and move on to the next note. Once you get used to the routines and the terms used to describe them, it is really very simple.

All that's needed is to code the eight bits of information for each note and upload the Robo sketch which has been written and debugged for you.

Just a word about the Arduino IDE software (Integrated Development Environment). It is open source software (which means that it's free and can used by anyone without worrying about patents or copyrights) and is used to write the sketches, compile them, edit and manage the files and bring up the serial monitor to debug the sketches. An updated version of the IDE is now available—download it to your PC according to the Arduino instructions. Since the Robo sketch has been written for you, there is no need to learn a great deal about C++ or about writing sketches. That said, writing a simple sketch to turn an LED on and off using Simon Monk's book is a worthwhile exercise and is recommended.

My experience with the Arduino IDE is very good and the new version is better yet. I have been mystified at times with error messages such as "Cannot find Com 3" when I was using Com 12 (disconnecting the USB cable and resetting the Mega and the PC resolved the problem)—some of the cryptic comments from the compiler are less than helpful to solve typing errors—but overall it is more than adequate for this project.

We will now look at the sheet music and the musical symbols that are used to tell the pianist (in our case, the coder) how to make our player piano play music.

Sheet Music and Musical Symbols

The first piano invented by Bartholomeo Cristofori in 1722, was a direct descendent of the harpsichord. It had 49 keys (four octaves) which grew to 61 keys (five octaves) by the late 1700's. By the early 1800's, motivated by composers like Beethoven, manufacturers built 73-key pianos. Then, about 150 years ago, pianos reached their present 88 keys (seven + octaves). The human ear has trouble assimilating higher or lower pitched notes, so that this range is not likely to be expanded.

Sheet music looks like the sample below. It can be bought at music stores or ordered online by looking up the name of the song. To understand the Robo sketch that we'll be using to direct the operation of the player piano, it's important to understand the symbols and the conventions used in sheet music.

Fig 4.1 – Sample Sheet Music. Beethoven's Fur Elise

Although we won't go into every symbol used in sheet music, we will describe all the basic ones as well as the ones that we will code in the Robo sketch.

Staffs

When we look at the sheet music written for the piano, we first notice that there are two sets of five lines and 4 spaces running across the page. They are called the "Staff." Every line and every space represents a different pitch for the notes. The pitch or the frequency of the note located on or between the lines increases as it is located on a higher line or space.

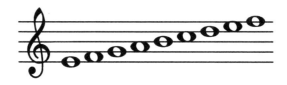

This is the treble staff. The treble clef (the large fancy symbol to the far left) shows the musician that the staff is treble. Since it curls around the G line, it is also called a G clef. The treble staff begins with the first note on the first line—this is an E. Each successive space and line is the next letter in the musical alphabet: it ranges from A to F. The 7 notes from G to F constitute one octave.

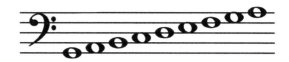

Pictured above is the bass staff (pronounced "base staff"), also known as an F clef because it locates the line F between its two dots. The bass staff uses the same musical alphabet as the treble staff but the letters start in different places. Instead of an E, the bottom note on the first line is a G and the last note on the top line is an A.

Measures

The vertical lines on the staff mark the measures. Measures are used to divide and organize the music. A fraction (such as 4/4) determines how many beats there are in a measure (in this case 4). The thick double bars mark the beginning and end of a piece of music. Measures are sometimes marked with sequential numbers to make navigating a piece of music easier. The first measure would be measure one, the second measure two and so on.

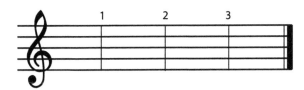

Ledger Lines

The ledger lines are found above and below the staffs. They provide the needed space to show notes that have a higher or lower pitch than the ones that can be shown on the staffs. They follow the same alphabet pattern that is used on the staff just as if there were more lines and spaces available. They are very useful because, at a glance, you can determine how many keys will be needed to play a certain piece of music. Most pop music will have at most two ledger lines but classical pieces may have six or more.

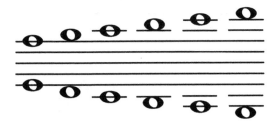

Clefs

On the left side of the top staff is a symbol known as the "Treble Clef" or "G Clef." It looks somewhat like a G and its center is located on the second line of the top staff, which makes the notes on that line have a pitch of "G."

On the left of the bottom staff, there is another symbol called the "Bass Clef" or the "F Clef" because its center and the semi-colon to its right are centered on the fourth line (counting from the bottom). The notes on that line have the pitch of an "F."

When the top staff and the bottom staff are joined by a brace, it turns the two staffs into a "Grand Staff" which contains all the notes for that musical selection. On the piano, the top staff notes are played mostly by the right hand and the bottom staff notes are played mostly by the left hand.

The Rhythm, Tempo or the Beat of the Music

3/4

When you tap your foot or clap your hands to the beat of a song, you are tapping in synch with the measures of the song. The duration of this recurring beat is determined by the fraction located on the first grand staff after the treble clef and the bass clef. Being a fraction, it has a numerator on top and a denominator on the bottom. The numerator tells us how many beats there are in each measure and the denominator tells us which note has the beat. In "Fur Elise" the song shown above, the fraction 3/4 tells us that there are 3 beats per measure and that the quarter note has the beat. Looking at the sheet music of "Fur Elise" again, notice that since the quarter note has the beat, you find 3 quarter notes in each measure (or the equivalent, 6 eighth notes or a half note and a quarter note since each of these groups have the same duration). On the first page of "Fur Elise", most notes are eighths and quarters with a single half note.

These simple fractions determining the beat, also known as time signatures, include 2/4 for two-step country music, 3/4 mostly for waltzes (also known as 3/4 time) and 4/4 for popular music.

The Notes and the Rests

The five notes shown on page 48 are called the naturals. They're played on the white keys and vary in duration. Compared to a quarter note which may have the beat, a whole note will last 4 times as long as the quarter note and a sixteenth note will have a duration of one fourth that of the quarter note.

The rests are places where the musician or coder does not play anything. Their symbols and their note equivalents are also shown above. On the first line, on the left, we see a whole note with its equivalent whole rest. On the right, we find a quarter note and its quarter rest. On the second line, we show a half note and a half rest on the left and an eighth note and an eighth rest on the right. Between the two lines we find the sixteenth note and its equivalent sixteenth rest. *(Diagram courtesy of Method behind the Music)*

The Accidentals

While it's known that the history of the accidentals (the black keys) dates back to the Middle Ages, the etymology of the name is a mystery to me. In any case, they are closely related to their natural equivalent note—the note that follows the symbol. In the diagram below, we see three symbols telling us that the note that follows is: either a sharp, a flat, or it negates the previous symbol. The first note is a sharp which raises the pitch of the note by one semitone (a half step higher than the natural next to it). The second note is a flat which reduces the pitch of the note by one semitone. The third symbol tells us to discontinue the action of either of the first two symbols. *(Diagram courtesy of Wikipedia)*

Notes with a Dot

The dot next to a note indicates that its duration is 50% greater than normal. The dotted note shown here has a duration half way between a quarter note and a half note.

Beamed Notes

The beam across the top of notes is the equivalent of putting a little flag on each note. The one shown below is for eighth-notes, if they were sixteenth-notes, there would be two horizontal beams to replace two little flags on each note.

Ties and Slurs

Ties and slurs are the arcs that indicate that the two connected notes are to be played or sung together as one note while adding their time duration. Ties (shown right) are for identical notes, while slurs are arcs used to connect notes of a different pitch.

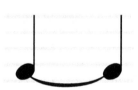

Dynamics of the Song

The intensity or volume of the notes can vary from very soft to "piano" in the middle, to very loud. The symbols go from *ppp* to *p* (piano), and from *p* to *fff* (fortissimo), very loud.

Chords

As the diagram shows, chords are played when several notes are shown in the same vertical position indicating that they are played simultaneously.

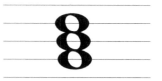

Metronome Mark

Maelzel's Metronome shown right indicates the tempo or beat of the music. In this case, exactly 120 quarters-notes fit into one minute of time.

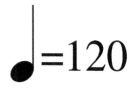

Each quarter note has, therefore, a duration of ½ second or 500 milliseconds. Since the tempo of the rendition is at the discretion of the musician, you seldom see this symbol in sheet music.

Sustain Symbol

Ped is the only symbol for sustain that I could find. It is rarely used. The musician determines when he wants to use sustain just as he decides on loudness and tempo. He could use it for the entire rendition or not use it all.

Other Symbols

There are many other musical symbols but you are not likely to run into them in the sheet music that you buy. If you do, check out Wiki under "List of Musical Symbols" where you will find many, many more.

About Notes and Octaves

From "The Sound of Music" we all know that there are 7 notes in an octave (the word "octave" relates to 8 but let's not get picky) before it starts over again. These 7 notes are: Do, Re, Mi, Fa, So, La, Si. On the sheet music for the piano, the notes are called: C, D, E, F, G, A, B. These are the naturals (the white keys). Between them there are 5 accidentals, the sharps or flats (black keys) which make up a total of 12 keys per octave.

Each time a new higher octave is played its first note has twice the frequency of the first note of the previous octave. For example, if we start playing an octave at middle C (also known as C4) which has a frequency of 261.6 Hz (Hertz or cycles per second) we will find that the next higher C note (C5) has a frequency of twice C4's frequency or 523.2 Hz.

Interestingly, when a piano is tuned (to 440 Hz with a pitch fork), it is the next A after middle C which controls the tuning of the entire piano. Then the other six A notes are adjusted to double or to one half of this frequency as we progress up or down the keyboard. All other notes are tuned to the harmonics of the A notes. Incidentally, player keyboards which are controlled by crystal oscillators, which have a fixed frequency never need to be tuned.

Master Chart for the Notes of the Player Piano

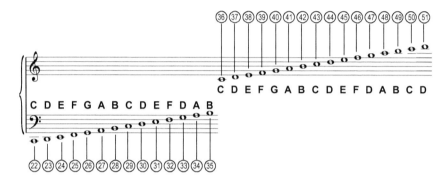

Fig 4.2 – Chart of the Ports and the White Notes

The chart above shows the two staffs with the note middle C on the ledger line between the staffs. (middle C is usually shown on the ledger line below the treble staff). Depending on your taste in music, activating 60 of the 76 available keys should be sufficient for your player piano as it was for me. While some light classical pieces such as Debussy's "Claire de Lune" clearly hit higher notes and need all the keys that are available, popular music seldom does. That is because popular music is often intended to be played on guitars, which have a range of only four octaves.

I hinted before that this player keyboard project could be simplified substantially if only about 50 notes were activated. This would be the case if only popular music were to be played, or if the songs to be played were mainly the melody accompanying a guitar player. We saw in the Wiki's Range of Musical Instruments that the guitar has a range of 4 octaves. This range would match a 50-note player keyboard perfectly. Even if only 50 keys were to be activated, a 61-key keyboard would be a better choice than an inexpensive 49- or 50-key keyboard.

When we get to wiring the control box and the solenoids, I intend to provide two master wiring charts: one for a full 76-note keyboard (which can also be used for the 60-key configuration) and one for a simplified 50-key keyboard. That should satisfy the classic buffs as well as the pop musicians. Meanwhile, the chart shown above provides some insight as to how the notes are selected. The chart shows the 30 white keys with their port numbers. The 20 black keys and their port numbers (the accidentals) are not shown on this chart.

Starting at middle C and going up in pitch we can see that middle C is activated by port 36. The highest pitched key that can be played in a 50-key configuration is a D, played by selecting port 51. Going down in pitch from middle C we can go to C2 (14 white keys away from middle C). C2 is activated when port 22 is selected. Since there are 2 unused ports (after allowing for the two ports needed for sustain and volume control), these ports could be added to the high or low pitch keys to provide some versatility in selecting music.

To code the accidentals, the sharps and the flats, we will have a chart referring to the port number of the white key and its relation to the port number of the accidental. More on this subject in Part 2.

We will be coding music in Chapter 14, but just to give you a feel for what Robo will need in order to activate the musical notes, let us look at the first note of "Fur Elise," which happens to be an E. From the diagram above, we see that this note has a port number of 45. This port number will be one of the eight items to be recorded in order to activate the E solenoid for the proper note duration.

Other information to be recorded includes whether it is a white or black note. By this time the coder will have decided on the beat of the song and whether the volume pedal or the sustain pedal needs to be activated, thereby providing 7 of the 8 bits of information needed by Robo. The last bit of information needed is whether this E note is a normal note or one that is part of a chord.

Summary of Chapter 4

In Chapter 4, we provided background notes on computers and the Arduino Mega in particular. We just touched on the methods for providing the needed information to the Mega computer so that it can select and activate the appropriate key for an appropriate time duration.

A list of the notes and musical symbols that we will use was described. These are needed to interpret the sheet music and translate this information for the Robo sketch.

The discussion of the notes and octaves lead us to a description of a master note chart. Using this chart makes it possible to select a port number that will activate the appropriate solenoid.

CHAPTER 5

The Electronic Circuits

Having reached the middle of Part 1, this is a good time to review what we have learned and done so far and also to describe what still needs to be done in the second half of Part 1.

We provided an overview of the entire project and selected a keyboard and an acceptable solenoid. The keyboard was modified to accept the mounting hardware for the solenoids that were modified to reduce their noise level. In Chapter 4 we learned all about the musical symbols that are found in sheet music.

In this chapter, we will describe the design and the operation of the four electronic circuits used in the project namely the solenoid drivers, the decoders for the black keys (not needed in the 50-key configuration), the volume control and the sustain circuits. These are the only electronic circuits needed to operate the player piano and each one has only a handful of components. With some necessary repetition in the descriptions, we will show how to mount the driver and decoder circuits in the control box in Chapter 6. In Chapter 7, we will wire these circuits to the solenoids. The wiring of the sustain and volume control functions will be described in this chapter.

The Solenoid Driver

Since as many as 76 keys may be activated, it pays to make sure that as few components as possible are used for each solenoid driver in order to reduce the clutter of wires and components.

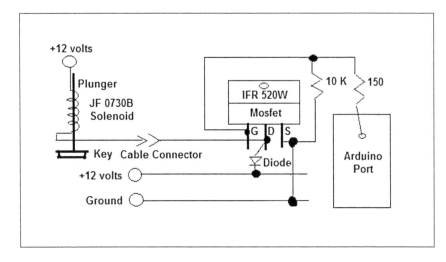

Fig. 5.1 – Mosfet Solenoid Driver Circuit

The schematic diagram above shows the driver circuit needed for each solenoid. The "push" solenoid on the left is shown with a plunger capable of depressing a black or a white key. One of the solenoid wires (there are two and they are interchangeable) is connected to the +12-volt supply. The 12-volt power is distributed to all the solenoids on a bus cable (#14 bare copper wire). The power comes from the control box over four grey wires, connected in parallel, in four different solenoid cables. When playing chords, several solenoids are activated simultaneously. We want to make sure that the 12-volt supply voltage does not drift down too much.

The other solenoid wire goes to the control box via one wire of the solenoid cable. It passes through a connector and goes to the middle pin of the IFR520 Mosfet switch. There can be as many as 76 such wires. They are soldered to the middle pin of the Mosfet from the bottom of the breadboard. As many as 76 wires are connected to the gates of the 76 Mosfets (left pin). As we will see in Chapter 7, they are soldered to a 150-ohm resistor on the top side of the breadboard.

The IFR520 is a common, inexpensive Mosfet power switch rated at 10 amps at 100 volts which is more than adequate for this job (many other electronic switches could also be used). When looking at the front of the Mosfet, the gate (which turns the switch on and off) is the pin on the left, the drain is in the middle and the source which is connected to ground is on the right.

The connection coming from the Arduino port (a chart showing the destination of all the port terminals will be provided in Chapter 7) has a 150 ohm (1/2 watt) resistor in series with the connection to the gate. The sturdier ½-watt resistor is used here because it doubles as a post for the wire connection going to the port. The resistor is used to protect the Arduino port in case of a short to ground or to the 12-volt supply. This same connection also has a 10,000 ohm (1/4 watt) resistor to ground. The purpose of this resistor is to avoid a condition whereby the gate and the port float (when they are neither fully turned on nor fully turned off) when power is first turned on. The Robo sketch has a routine which turns off all the ports but the floating condition could happen before the sketch starts running. As unlikely as this may seem, it does happen and causes the solenoids to activate seemingly on their own. When the gate is driven by the decoder (for the black keys), this resistor is not really needed since the output of the decoder is either high or low. I left it in as a safety precaution in case of an open circuit in the wiring.

The last component to be installed is the diode. Its purpose is to protect the Mosfet. When the Mosfet switch turns off, a large voltage spike is generated in the inductive coil of the solenoid. The spike is sufficiently large to exceed the specification of the Mosfet. The diode, a common 1N7004 component, will not allow the voltage to exceed 13 volts. Unlike the resistors which have no polarity and can be installed in either direction, the polarity of the diode must be observed. The wire near the silver band must be attached to the +12-volt supply as shown in the driver circuit schematic (Fig 5.1)

PC Boards and Breadboards

There seems to be an infinite variety of printed circuit boards and breadboards of all sizes and shapes. The better ones have "printed through holes," meaning that the holes provide an electrical connection from the top of the board to the bottom of the board. This makes for a very strong bond once a wire is soldered to it.

Inexpensive breadboards on the other hand, come in larger sizes but the "pads" (the small copper circles around the hole) can easily be scratched off or burned off if too much heat is used when soldering wires to it. Nevertheless, Radio Shack's 4 ½ by 6 1/4 is used here because it has approximately the right size and provides the large amount of circuit board real estate needed. Two boards are needed; each one has 55 x 40 holes for a total of 4400 holes spaced .1 inches apart. Approximately 45 holes are available for each Mosfet driver. If each Mosfet is allocated 1/2 inch (5 holes) then 8 holes are available between rows.

The pictures on the following page, which require a good deal of imagination, show a top view and a bottom view of two Mosfet drivers. They include the drivers' three components as well as the +12-volt bus and the ground bus, the input wires to the Arduino port (on top) and the output wiring to the solenoid (on the bottom). The connection from the Arduino port (white keys) or from the decoder (for the black keys) is soldered to the end of the 150-ohm resistor which then goes to the gate of the Mosfet (left pin). On the bottom side, the cable connection attaches to the middle pin of the Mosfet as well as to the anode of the diode (the end that does not have a ring). Finally, the 10,000 ohm resistor is connected from the gate to the right-hand pin to ground. All the +12-volt connections form a bus and all the ground connections form another bus.

2 Mosfet Drivers

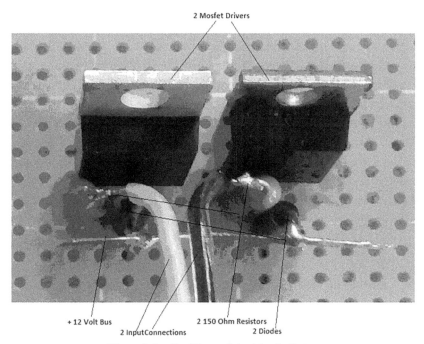

+ 12 Volt Bus

2 InputConnections

2 150 Ohm Resistors

2 Diodes

Photo 5.1 – Top View of the Mosfet Driver

Ground Bus   2 10K resistors

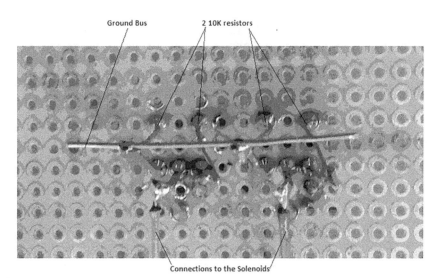

Connections to the Solenoids

Photo 5.2 – Bottom View of the Mosfet Driver

Solenoid Drivers Needed for Three Different Configurations

We have mentioned that depending on the builder/musician's taste in music, he may not want to utilize the full 76 keys of the keyboard. Three possibilities are discussed here along with their implementation. To reproduce classical piano music, the drivers to all 76 keys should be implemented. For popular music that is also played on the guitar, there is no need to exceed the guitar's range of four octaves. In this case, 50 keys are adequate. For my own taste, which encompasses popular music, country music and light classical such as Beethoven's "Fur Elise", I am implementing a 60-key configuration. All configurations use the same Robo sketch and software

- So, how many rows of eight drivers do we need? If all 76 keys (45 white and 31 black keys) are implemented, the answer is 6 rows for the white keys and 4 rows for the black keys (there will be one spare). Two of the three drivers left over from the white key array will be used to implement the volume control and sustain functions. The last one is a spare.

- If 60 keys are to be activated, as we are doing in this book, with 35 white keys and 25 black keys, the answer is 5 rows for the white keys and 3 rows for the black keys. The rows are spaced 8 pins apart as in the 76-key configuration. The 5 extra keys from the white key array will be allocated as follows: One for the 25th black key driver, two for the volume and sustain circuits and 2 spare positions.

- If a simplified 50-key configuration is to be implemented, with 30 white keys (4 rows) and 20 black keys (3 rows), the answer is a total of 7 rows with 52 drivers and 4 spare positions. The two drivers not used for the keys are used to activate the volume and sustain circuits. In this simplified configuration, there is no need for a decoder circuit since every driver is activated by one of Arduino's 54 ports.

Operation of the Decoder

We have hinted at the need of a decoder (also known as a demulti-plexer) to select and operate the black keys. Let us review what we are trying to do and why this is necessary.

- The Arduino Mega has a maximum of 54 ports

- We may want to activate as many as 76 keys, 45 white keys and 31 black keys.

- A port is needed for each white key because they are often part of a chord in which several white keys and, occasionally, a black key are activated simultaneously.

- The black keys on the other hand, are seldom activated with another black key to form a chord (I have not seen them called out in my sheet music)

Consequently, it is possible to select and activate the black keys from the output of a decoder which requires only 5 ports in order to select any one of the 31 black keys. This keeps our port count to 50, yet, we are capable of activating all 76 solenoids. There are other ways to solve this problem such as adding a second Arduino Mega with an additional 54 ports (one Mega for the white keys and one Mega for the black keys) but the decoder seems to be the most cost effective solution.

The SN74154 Decoder

The SN74154 is the standard, old style TTL computer logic device that is used to decode 4 lines of binary coded inputs into one of sixteen mutually exclusive outputs. This means that if you code say, output port #4 in binary (0100) and put this coded word on the input lines of the 74154, output line #4 will be activated and all other outputs will be deactivated. But, as we will see, there is a problem with this chip. Before solving that problem, let us learn how to code port numbers in binary.

Binary Numbering System

We have mentioned that computers are dumb in that they only know 1's and 0's. In fact, they can handle much larger numbers when they are coded properly. For example, if the number 100 is written in the binary numbering system it means 4. Only 1s and 0s are used, yet we have a number greater than a one. We don't need to know much more to complete this project but if you are interested in reading more about binary and octal numbering systems you can find it explained online in Wikipedia.

The chart below shows the 31 black keys that we want to activate numbered in our familiar Decimal numbering system as well as in the Binary and Octal numbering systems.

Notice that after decimal 7, the next number is 10 in both the binary and the octal system (there is no 8). After the next octave of numbers, we get to 20 in both binary and octal. Therefore, if we want to activate the 7th black key we will code it octal 7 (binary 00111) but if we want to activate the 15th black key, its code will be octal 17 (binary 01111). The 25th black key which is 31 in octal will have a binary code of 11001. To code the black keys, we will provide a conversion chart for these notes labeled with their port number in binary to avoid mistakes.

Decimal	Binary	Octal	Decimal	Binary	Octal
1	00001	1	17	10001	21
2	00010	2	18	10010	22
3	00011	3	19	10011	23
4	00100	4	20	10100	24
5	00101	5	21	10101	25
6	00110	6	22	10110	26
7	00111	7	23	10111	27
8	01000	10	24	11000	30
9	01001	11	25	11001	31
10	01010	12	26	11010	32
11	01011	13	27	11011	33
12	01100	14	28	11100	34
13	01101	15	29	11101	35
14	01110	16	30	11110	36
15	01111	17	31	11111	37
16	10000	20			

Fig 5.2 – Decimal/Binary/Octal Conversion Chart

A problem with the SN74154 Decoder

The problem that we mentioned with the standard SN74154, 4 to 16 decoder, is that its output is Low (ground) when the port number is decoded.

Since we need a High output (+5 volts) to activate the gate of the Mosfet driver, 31 inverters would have to be added to the drive circuits to invert the output of the SN74154. That requires a lot of wiring. There is a newer pair of decoders, the MC14514 and the MC14515 where the designer has a choice of High or Low outputs. We will use the MC14514 with the positive outputs. These IC's (integrated circuits) are a little more expensive and more difficult to find than the standard variety but it is a worthwhile trade-off.

The Decoder Circuit

The 3 circuits that we have discussed previously were made of discreet components (diodes and resistors), but this decoder computer circuit is assembled with integrated circuits (IC's also known as "chips"). IC's are more than 50 years old. They have evolved gradually from simple DIP's (dual-in-line package) to LSI's (large scale integration) models with thousands of transistors to today's 3D chips and computer systems on a chip. The material is different, the packaging is new and the performance has improved by a factor of millions.

Despite these great advances, Moore's law states that performance will continue to double every two years, although we have seen that there is still a need for discreet components as in the speaker modification. We will also use one DIP (the inverter) and one LSI circuit, the MC14514 decoder in the decoder circuit. The ATmega1280 microprocessor is a good example of large scale integration. It contains millions of transistors and is surface mounted on the Arduino computer board.

Circuit Diagram for the Decoders

The decoder circuit diagram below shows the two decoders and the inverter (only one of its six circuits is used). The power pin wiring, the inputs to the decoders and the outputs from the decoders are shown. Five outputs from the Arduino's ports (ports 5, 6, 7, 8, and 9) are connected to the inputs of the two MC14514. Each unit can decode 4 binary bits into 16 individual outputs but provisions are made in the device to expand to 32 outputs by adding a second decoder. We can accomplish this by connecting the most significant digit from the Arduino port (port 5) to pin 23 (the inhibit pin) of one of the two decoders then we reverse the polarity of this same signal with an inverter and connect it to the inhibit input of the other decoder, thereby doubling the number of decoded outputs. The outputs of the two decoders go to the input gates of the 31 Mosfet drivers. Note that output zero is not used because there is no Mosfet # 0.

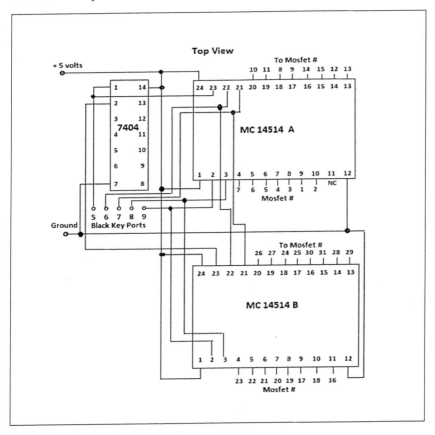

Fig 5.3 – Decoder Circuit for the Black Keys

For this application the strobe pin is always at +5 volts because the speed of this device is many orders of magnitudes faster than what is needed. The 5K resistors connected to output ports 5 to 9 avoid the floating condition that we mentioned before. The power pins of the decoders are pins 12 and 24 while the power pins of the inverter are pins 7 and 14. Ground and + 5 volts which come from the Mega are connected to these pins.

That's all there is to it! Let's decode a note, say, 25 octal. We look on the conversion chart and find that its binary equivalent is 10101. The most significant digit is the "1" on the left which means the output of port 5 is high. After going through the inverter the signal will become Low (ground) on pin 23 of decoder B thereby activating decoder B and inhibiting decoder A.

Now that the correct decoder is activated, we look at the other 4 data bits: 0101 which are activated. The data sheet for the MC14514, available online from "ON Semiconductors" tells us in the "Decode Truth Table" that 0101 produces a positive output on line 5. Add 20 octal, (16 decimal) because the output is from decoder B and, voila, the correct answer: 25 octal.

Sustain and Volume Control Circuits

The design of these two simple circuits is described below and the wiring of the components will also be shown here although most of the wiring of the control box is reserved for Chapter 7.

The Sustain Circuit

Most pianos have 3 pedals that are used to add special effects to the music. One is the sustain pedal on the right, another is the soft/volume reduction pedal on the left. The function of the third, middle pedal sometimes depends on the make of the piano, but generally, it is also used to sustain the note being played. It has little use and the sheet music seldom refers to it. It is not implemented here.

In a piano, the sustain pedal mechanically disengages the damper which normally stops the piano wires from vibrating excessively. The "soft" pedal decreases the volume by shifting the hammers closer to the strings. In some pianos, it can also allow the hammers to strike only one of the piano wires for its particular key rather than the normal two or three.

In the Yamaha keyboard, when the sustain pedal, which is part of the "survival kit," is depressed, sustain is activated. It simulates the operation of the piano's sustain pedal by extending the length of the notes. Taking the sustain pedal apart reveals that when it is plugged into the sustain connector in back of the keyboard, the circuit which is normally closed opens when the pedal is depressed. Simulating this action with a relay controlled by the Arduino is a simple task. The diagram below shows how the sustain function is activated from a spare Mosfet driver.

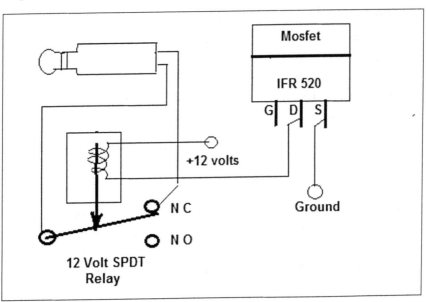

Fig 5.4 – The Sustain Circuit

As we can see, using one of the solenoid drivers, the sustain relay mounted on the left circuit board is activated in the same manner as the solenoids are activated. We use a normally closed contact of the relay to replace the normally closed contact of the foot pedal. As shown on the diagram, the two wires from the sustain connector are soldered to the common and to the normally closed contacts of the relay.

When a signal from computer port 18 activates the relay, it opens the sustain circuit (just as the pedal would do). The player piano remains in sustain mode as long as the relay remains energized.

The Robo sketch has the necessary code to interpret the 1 that is placed in the sustain command location (one of the 8 bits of information provided for each note). The sustain function remains active until a subsequent note with a "0" in the sustain location turns it off.

Volume Control Circuit Diagram

The circuit below shows the two wires going to each of the two speakers. To reduce the volume of the speakers it is necessary to insert a resistor of an appropriate size in series with the speaker coil. A potentiometer (basically an adjustable resistor) can also be used instead of a resistor to make this volume control variable.

Since at normal volume level, there is zero resistance in series with the speaker coil, this added resistor must be shorted out for normal volume and opened for reduced volume.

The three components—the double pole/double throw relay and two 10 ohm, 1-watt resistors that I used—are mounted on a small 1.5 by 1.5 inch breadboard circuit board which is then mounted in a convenient location under the top cover of the Yamaha keyboard.

Note that there is a bug in the Yamaha sustain circuit as described on page 11 of the owner's manual. The operation of sustain can become reversed: an open circuit instead of a closed circuit causes the sustain feature to operate. This happens when the power to the Yamaha is turned on while the foot switch is depressed (sustain is turned on). To restore the operation to normal, turn power on again while the foot switch is depressed.

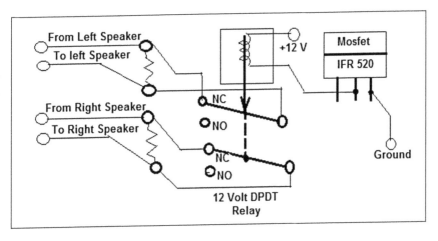

Fig 5.5 – The Volume Control Circuit

To open the Yamaha cover, remove the 21 screws that keep it in place. I did this job on a bed for safety's sake and so as not to scratch the plastic. There is no need to disconnect any cables to expose the speaker wires, just open the top as if it were on a hinge. Remove the red wire from the speaker and attach it (solder it) to either end of the resistor. Attach a new stranded wire (# 22 or speaker wire) from the other end of the resistor to the terminal from which the red wire was removed. You have now put a series resistor in the speaker circuit. The volume will be reduced. Experiment with the value of the resistor until you are happy with the reduced volume. The second speaker is rewired the same way.

To make sure that the speaker operates at full volume when the relay has not been activated or is disconnected from the speaker circuit, the resistors have to be shorted out. This is done by wiring the normally closed (NC) contacts of the relay to each end of the resistors. NC contacts are closed when the relay is not energized or is disconnected from its source.

The last thing to be done is to provide the operating power to the coil of the relay. A connector similar to the one used for the sustain circuit is installed in the back of the Yamaha. I would use one smaller than the ¼ inch plug and socket used for sustain simply to avoid mixing them up. The two wires from the plug go to +12 volts and to the middle terminal of the Mosfet driver as it is shown on the diagram (the +12 volt is usually connected to the center terminal) The two wires from the socket go to each side of the coil of the relay are also shown on the diagram.

The reduced volume operation works the same way as the sustain function. Low volume is coded as one of the eight bits of information provided for each note. The Robo sketch interprets this information and activates the port 19 Mosfet which energizes the low volume relay that we just installed. Low volume will stay active until another note with full volume is coded and interpreted by Robo.

Summary of Chapter 5

This very busy chapter described the three electronic circuits used in this project as well as the computer logic circuitry that is used to decode and select the correct driver for the 31 black keys (the sharps and flats also known as the accidentals).

Each key, black or white needs a solenoid driver to activate its solenoid to play the note. When all the keys of the Yamaha keyboard are implemented, 76 solenoids and drivers are needed. We have seen that depending on the builder's taste in music fewer keys may be implemented such as 60 keys as we are doing in this book or 50 keys if popular music is mostly played.

When 50 keys are implemented, which covers the same four octave range as the guitar, there is no need for a decoder since the Arduino computer has 54 ports. Each of the 50 notes can therefore be activated directly from a port.

The solenoid driver, the volume control and the sustain control are simple circuits made of discreet components. The sustain circuit is mounted in an empty area at the top of the left breadboard in the control box. The volume control circuit, on the other hand, is installed near the speakers inside the body of the Yamaha keyboard.

Prior to explaining the design of the decoder, the binary and octal numeric systems were discussed briefly with references to online resources for further study. The same thing was done to review the evolution of computer logic over the years.

A diagram and an explanation of the workings of the decoder circuit were presented. The example of decoding port 25 was explained in detail more to prove that it can be done rather than with the expectation that the reader needs to learn how to do it.

The next two chapters will explain how to mount and wire these circuits. Wiring charts will be provided for the three configurations that we have discussed in this chapter.

CHAPTER 6

Populating the Control Box

Dividing up the Space

Before describing (in the next chapter) how to wire the circuits that
we designed in Chapter 5, it's important show the location of the
components for the each of the 3 configurations. Photo 7.1 provides a
good visual representation of the main components.

A good deal of planning went into dividing up the space in the control
box. Some of it came from trial and error, but after three tries I feel pretty
sure that everything fits properly. The box was too small on my first
attempt. This one, 10 inches by 8 inches and 2 inches high, accommodates
the various circuit boards, cables and connectors very efficiently.

First, we install the two 4.5 by 6.25 inch Radio Shack breadboards. The
copper lands go on the bottom and the components go on top. The ¼
inch spaces (which have no lands) between the two boards are super-
imposed and the boards are bolted together with two 6/32 nuts and bolts.
This reduces the overall width of the two boards by a 1/4 inch to 8.75
inches. The boards are attached to the bottom of the box on three ½
inch nylon stand-offs using 6/32 nuts and bolts. The boards are located
¼ inch from the back side of the box and ½ inch from the right side of
the box.

Next, the Arduino Mega is located at the front right-hand corner of the
box, 1/8 inch from the right side of the box. This location allows the
UBS cable and the 12-volt power source cable to fit through the right
side of the box and plug into the Mega. It is mounted on two 3/8 inch

nylon standoffs with two small diameter 4-40, ¾ inch long screws on the front part of the right-hand breadboard. A one inch oval hole is cut out of the cover to allow the Mega's LED's to be viewed without removing the cover.

We have mentioned that the wires from the Arduino ports and the decoders are soldered to one of the leads (cut to a 1/4 inch) of the 150-ohm resistors which act as connecting posts. The other 3 components namely the Mosfet, the 10,000-ohm resistor and the diode are also mounted topside. To solder the leads from the cable connectors to the middle pin of the Mosfets without removing the breadboards from their standoffs, it would be necessary to cut a large window out of the bottom of the box and cover the hole with a thin piece of Plexiglass. Alternately, if done with great care and with nimble fingers, it is possible to solder the cables and connectors to the Mosfets and install the whole package in the box. Be sure to measure the length of the cables carefully and to label them.

Cable Connections from the Outside of the Control Box

The back side and the right side of the box are drilled out to accommodate a variety of cables. The front and left side are cut out to accommodate the solenoid cable connectors as shown in Photos 2.5 and 7.1.

The back side of the box requires two ¾ inch holes with rubber grommets to avoid having the cables rub against the sharp edges of the aluminum. As seen in photo 7.1, the left-hand hole lines up with the 12-volt socket which brings the power to the control box from an in-line power supply. The second hole, 2 inches to the right, accommodates the two cables going to the back of the Yamaha keyboard for the volume control and the sustain functions. The sustain relay used to activate this function is mounted near the top of the left-hand breadboard.

On the right side of the control box there are three holes that line up with the Arduino Mega. The one closest to the front of the control box is the place where the USB cable plugs in. It sticks out past the side of the control box by about 1/8 inch. It is a square hole. A ½ inch round hole is drilled first and then filed to make it square. Make sure that it is large enough to install and remove the Arduino board which will have to be raised and tipped to clear the mounting posts.

Another large hole is needed to bring outside power to the Arduino Mega when the USB cable is not plugged in. The outside power (usually a 9-volt battery) can range from 5 to 12 volts. In our case, it is connected to the 12-volt supply. A ¾ inch hole with grommet is adequate for the plug as long as it lines up properly with the Mega's socket. A smaller, ¼ inch hole with a grommet is located just north of the Mega's socket to bring the +12-volt power to the Arduino board. Its source is at the top of the left-hand breadboard. Two 10-ohm, 2-watt resistors are placed in series with the 12-volt circuit to reduce the voltage to approximately 8 volts. Without these resistors, the Mega's 5-volt voltage regulator overheats.

Two more 5/16 inch holes and one 3/16 inch hole are drilled in the right-hand side of the box. Two miniature toggle switches protrude through these holes. One is used to turn the +12-volt supply on and off. A red LED indicating that power is on is located near the switch. The other switch operates momentarily to master reset the Arduino.

These three components are mounted on a thin aluminum plate 2 inches by 1 inch and attached inside to the right side of the control box with 2 self-tapping screws. The idea is that in case the breadboards have to be removed from the control box, the plate with the switches can be unscrewed from the box without unsoldering wires.

Solenoid Cable Connections

To implement a full-blown 76-key control box, 10 cables are needed from the solenoids to the Mosfets. The arithmetic goes like this: there are 45 white keys. An array of 6 rows of Mosfet drivers with 8 drivers in each row is implemented. To make the wiring reasonably neat and easy to follow, we use eight conductors from a nine wire cable for each row. The extra wire in each cable can be a spare or be one of four wires used to bring the 12-volt power to the solenoid's 12-volt bus. Four cables in which eight of the nine conductors are used, are provided to connect the 31 black key solenoids to their respective Mosfet drivers. The drivers are arranged in an array of four rows of eight drivers. The cable connectors are located in the left front side of the control box.

As seen in the pictures of the control box, six of the 10 cable connectors are mounted on the left side of the control box and four connectors are mounted in the front of the box. I bought six 6-foot extension cables and cut them to the appropriate length to reach the connectors of the white keys. There was more than enough cabling left for the four cables going to the black keys. They can be used but keep in mind that these connectors are of the opposite gender. Therefore, we have six male connectors which are called plugs DB-9P and four female connectors called sockets DB-9S. The terminals in these connectors are 1/10 inches apart which is much more space than is available in miniature cable connectors. That said, be aware that it is not easy to solder the wires in place. A fine tip is needed for your soldering iron.

Color Coded Wires

A nice feature of these cables (the CB-397 extension cables listed in Chapter 8) is that the wires are color-coded, and the wire size is number 30 stranded. They have the same color-code sequence as the resistors do. The chart below shows the color-code of the conductors and their associated connector position.

1 = Black	6 = Green
2 = Brown	7 = Blue
3 = Red	8 = Violet
4 = Orange	9 = Gray
5 = Yellow	10 = White

The markings on the resistors actually start at 0, black being a 0, but they follow the same sequence as shown here. There are a number of limericks designed to help you remember this color-code. One version, not the most popular but appropriate for a family book, goes like this: Bad Beer Rots Our Young Guts But Vodka Goes Well.

Populating the Breadboards

The 76-Key Configuration

Now that we have a home for the Arduino and the two breadboards in the control box (left-hand for the white keys and right-hand for the black keys), let us see how we can populate them with Mosfet drivers and their associated components to activate as many as 76 keys. We will show four diagrams: two for the 76- and 60-key configurations and two for the 50-key configurations. In each case, there will be a left-hand board and a right-hand board. Note that the two boards overlap in the middle.

The "o"s in the diagrams, which are not to scale, represent the holes surrounded by the pads that are located 1/10 inch on center in the breadboards. Each row of "o"s represents about 1 1/2 rows of pads in the breadboards. The black horizontal bars represent the Mosfet drivers. Since there are 40 horizontal holes in the breadboard, we can allow five holes per Mosfet for each row of eight Mosfets. Each Mosfets requires three holes, which means that there are two holes between Mosfets, the ideal spacing. Horizontally, the location of the Mosfets could not be better. We will use this horizontal spacing of 8 Mosfets per row connected to an 8-conductor cable for all configurations.

Left-Hand Breadboard

Vertically, in the left-hand board (Fig 6.1), we need 6 rows of Mosfets to accommodate the 45 white key drivers. As shown, there are 3 empty spaces in the bottom row. The 6 rows of Mosfets spaced 8 rows apart require 41 rows of pads for the Mosfets. We need three empty rows of pads on the bottom for the components. This leaves 11 empty rows on top for other components namely the sustain relay and the 12-volt receptacle. The diagrams do not show all the rows of pads. They are used mainly to indicate the difference between configurations.

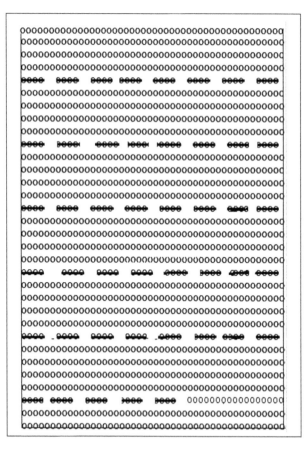

Fig 6.1 – Left-Hand Board for the 76-Key Configuration

Right-Hand Breadboard

The right-hand breadboard for the 76-key configuration is shown below in Fig 6.2. It has 31 Mosfets in 4 rows with one space left over. On the top, there is room for the two MC14514 decoders and one 7004 inverter. Note that the bottom row must be placed no closer than one inch from the bottom edge of the board. The reason is that the board must support and fit under the Arduino computer board. The Mosfets drivers for the black keys are also mounted eight per row and the rows are also 8 holes on center vertically.

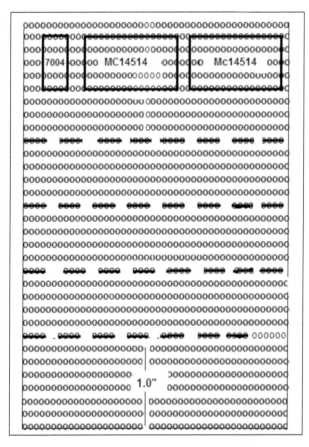

Fig 6.2 – Right-Hand Board for the 76-Key Configuration

60-Key Configuration

The left-hand and right-hand breadboards used for the 60-key configuration, which we implement in this book, are very similar to the above (the diagrams are not repeated). There are only 35 white keys instead of 45 so that the left-hand board has five rows of Mosfets instead of six (with five spaces left over). The vertical distance between rows was kept at eight but it could have been increased to 10 holes. Instead of 31 black keys there are only 25 in the 60-key configuration. The right-hand board has only 3 rows of Mosfet drivers spaced 10 holes apart. The 25th driver is located in the top row of the left-hand board where the five spare spaces are located.

50-Key Configuration

Shown on the following pages in Figs 6.3 and 6.4 are the diagrams for the 50-key configuration. This is the simplified configuration in which both the white and the black keys are driven directly from the 54 Arduino ports without the need of decoder computer logic. In this configuration there are 30 white keys and 20 black keys. As the diagrams below show, only 4 rows of Mosfets are needed in the left-hand board (with 2 spares) and 3 rows of Mosfets in the right-hand board (with 4 spares). The rows can be separated by 12 holes.

When it comes to doing the wiring, separate wiring charts will be provided for the 50-key configuration without the decoder logic since it is substantially different from the other two configurations.

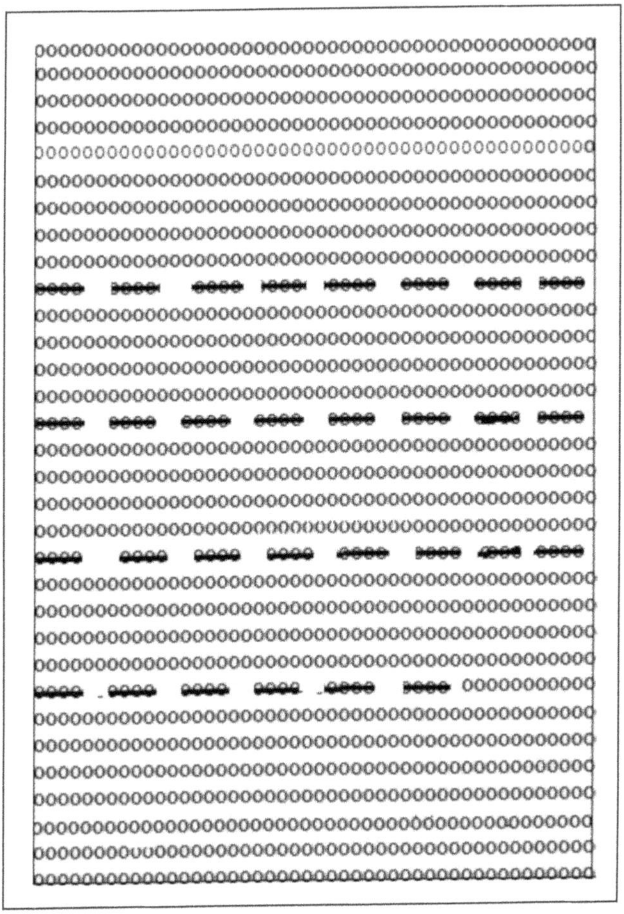

Fig 6.3 – Left-Hand Board for the 50-Key Configuration

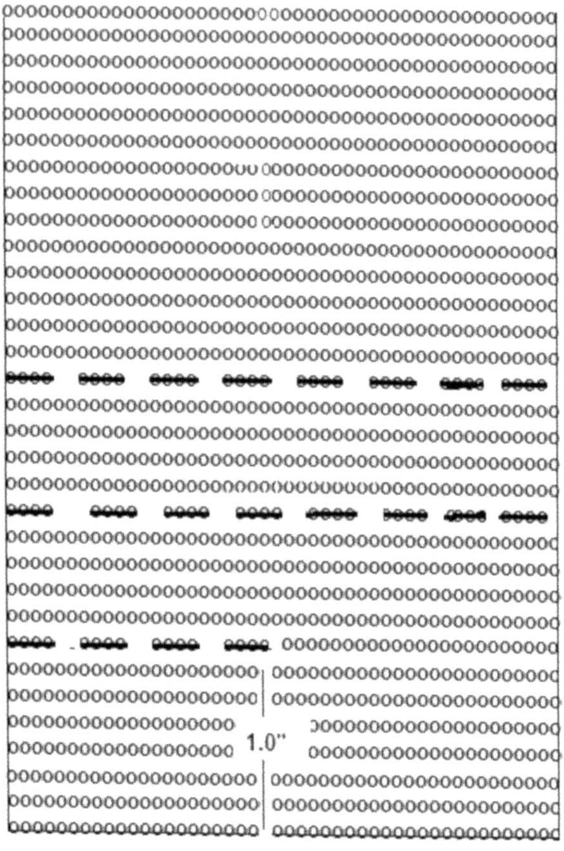

Fig 6.4 – Right-Hand Board for the 50-Key Configuration

Summary of Chapter 6

Chapter 6 details the construction of the control box including mounting the Aduino Mega, the two breadboards, the ten (or less) cable connectors and drilling a number of holes for the power cables.

When populating the breadboards, the location of the electronic components is described for various configurations. These are the full 76-key configuration, the 60-key configuration implemented in this book and the simplified 50-key configuration.

CHAPTER 7

Wiring the Control Box

Solenoid Wiring: White Keys (76- and 60-Key Configuration)

Generally, at this point, we would show a series of schematic diagrams from which to wire the devices. In this case, because there are so few circuits that are repeated as many as 76 times, a better approach is to generate listings which show the point to point wiring of the circuits. We will generate separate listings for the white and black keys since their circuits are different.

The listing below (Fig 7.1) is used for the 45 or 35 white keys of the 76- or 60-key configurations. In the 60-key configuration, we will indicate which keys are not used when discussing the wiring. We will always start at middle C and decide just how many white keys, of higher or lower pitch, are to be activated. For a 60-key configuration it might be 17 keys on each side of middle C (35 white keys in total). For a 50-key configuration it might be 14 lower pitched keys and 15 higher pitched keys from middle C (30 white keys in total). More on wiring the 50-key configuration later.

Using the first key as an example, we see that we are wiring the solenoid of white key #1—it is musical note E and we are using cable A to the control box. Of the 9 wires in cable A, we are connecting its black wire to the solenoid. Cable A plugs into connector A at the control box.

Master Wiring Chart: White Keys (60- &76-Key Configs)

White Key #	Note	Cable # Color	Connect # & Pin	Port #	Mosfet #
#1	E	A- Black	A Pin 1	#20	#1
#2	F	A- Brown	A Pin 2	#1	#2
#3	G	A- Red	A Pin 3	#2	#3
#4	A	A- Orang	A Pin 4	#3	#4
#5	B	A- Yellow	A Pin 5	#4	#5
#6	C2	A- Green	A Pin 6	#22	#6
#7	D	A- Blue	A Pin 7	#23	#7
#8	E	A- Violet	A Pin 8	#24	#8
#9	F	B- Black	B Pin 1	#25	#9
#10	G	B- Brown	B Pin 2	#26	#10
#11	A	B- Red	B Pin 3	#27	#11
#12	B	B- Orang	B Pin 4	#28	#12
#13	C3	B- Yellow	B Pin 5	#29	#13
#14	D	B- Green	B Pin 6	#30	#14
#15	E	B- Blue	B Pin 7	#31	#15
#16	F	B- Violet	B Pin 8	#32	#16
#17	G	C- Black	C Pin 1	#33	#17
#18	A	C- Brown	C Pin 2	#34	#18
#19	B	C- Red	C Pin 3	#35	#19
#20	Md C4	C- Orang	C Pin 4	#36	#20
#21	D	C- Yellow	C Pin 5	#37	#21
#22	E	C- Green	C Pin 6	#38	#22
#23	F	C- Blue	C Pin 7	#39	#23
#24	G	C- Violet	C Pin 8	#40	#24
#25	A	D- Black	D Pin 1	#41	#25
#26	B	D- Brown	D Pin 2	#42	#26
#27	C5	D- Red	D Pin 3	#43	#27
#28	D	D- Orang	D Pin 4	#44	#28
#29	E	D- Yellow	D Pin 5	#45	#29
#30	F	D- Green	D Pin 6	#46	#30
#31	G	D- Blue	D Pin 7	#47	#31
#32	A	D- Violet	D Pin 8	#48	#32
#33	B	E- Black	E Pin 1	#49	#33
#34	C6	E- Brown	E Pin 2	#50	#34
#35	D	E- Red	E Pin 3	#51	#35
#36	E	E- Orang	E Pin 4	#52	#36
#37	F	E- Yellow	E Pin 5	#53	#37
#38	G	E- Green	E Pin 6	#10	#38
#39	A	E- Blue	E Pin 7	#11	#39
#40	B	E- Violet	E Pin 8	#12	#40
#41	C7	F- Black	F Pin 1	#13	#41
#42	D	F- Brown	F Pin 2	#14	#42
#43	E	F- Red	F Pin 3	#15	#43
#44	F	F- Orang	F Pin 4	#16	#44
#45	G	F- Yellow	F Pin 5	#17	#45

Fig 7.1 – Master Wiring Chart for the White Keys

We have seen that the color coding used for resistors (and other electronic components) indicates that black is wire #1 and that it is connected to pin one of its connector. Then, if we wire pin one of the mating connector to the middle pin (the drain) of Mosfet #1 we will have completed the circuit from Mosfet #1 to drive solenoid #1 which activates white key #1.

Continuing with the Mosfet wiring, this time from the left-hand pin (the gate) of the Mosfet, the chart tells us to connect a wire from the 150-ohm resistor to the appropriate port of the Arduino in this case, port 20. Logically, we should have used port 0 but we decided to leave port 0 unused so that when pauses are programmed in the coding of the music, we could write six zeros for the port number. The use of the number 0 instead of 1 for the first number of a series is not unusual in computer electronics although it is admittedly confusing.

I'll provide another example. Middle C is key #20. One of the two wires from solenoid #20 goes to connector C (pin 4) to cable C's orange wire. From pin 4 of connector C, the wire continues to the drain of Mosfet 20. The gate circuit starts at port #36 with a wire that goes to the 150 resistor connected to the left pin of the Mosfet.

Notice the nomenclature—it all relates back to the key. For instance, the solenoid that drives white key #5 is solenoid 5. The Mosfet driver which activates solenoid 5 is Mosfet 5. But the port number assigned to this key is not related to 5 and the location of the Mosfet in its array has no relation to its number. For example, middle C is white key # 20, its associated solenoid and Mosfet are # 20 but its port # is 36 and, in a 50-key configuration, Mosfet 20 is located in the fifteenth position in the array.

In the 60-key configuration implemented in this book, white keys 1 and 2 are not used and neither are white keys 38 to 45. There are no solenoids mounted on the bar to drive these keys consequently, there is no need to install or wire the associated 10 Mosfet drivers. Simply cross off these ten entries from the master chart.

I should mention that of the 6 cables that I bought from "All Electronics" one of the cables did not follow the color code standard. The wire colors were pretty well scrambled. Be sure to check the cable wires rather than assume that they will follow the color code. What's important is that key #1 is activated by Mosfet #1. If it happens that, say, a yellow wire goes to pin one of the cable no harm is done by using that wire.

The vitally important connection to be made is for a Mega port to activate the correct black or white key. Which Mosfet driver is used or which wire or connector pin is used, does not matter. The listing shown here is one way to perform these connections in an orderly manner.

I had enough left-over color-coded wires when I cabled the solenoids to run the wires from the connector pins to the Mosfet drains with the left-over wires. For the connection from the gate of the Mosfet to the port, I used solid #22 wire of 4 different colors and made 4-conductor cables by taping them together. It is important that the wire that goes to the ports fits snuggly in the Arduino Mega's port connector. Number 22 solid wire is fine as it is. It can also be tinned since it adds only one or two thousands to the diameter of the wire. Number 24 wire is too fine for a good fit. Another way to get a tight fit for the port connector wires is to insert a header (available at All Electronics) in the port connector and solder the Mosfet wires (any size will do) to the appropriate header pin.

Solenoid Wiring of the Black Keys (76- and 60-Key Configs)

As we know, the black keys in the 76- and 60-key configurations use a decoder, but the decoder is not necessary in the 50-key configuration. Two listings are presented for the black keys configuration. They are Fig 7.2 with the decoder for the 76- and 60-key configurations and Fig 7.3 B which lists the black keys of the 50-key configuration.

Master Wiring Chart for Black Keys (60- & 76-Key Configs)

Black Key #	Note	Cable # Color	Connect & Pin #	Port # Code	Decoder	Mosfet #
#1	F#/Gb	G- Black	G Pin # 1	00001	A #9	#1
#2	G#/Ab	G- Brown	G Pin # 2	00010	A #10	#2
#3	A#/Bb	G- Red	G Pin # 3	00011	A #8	#3
#4	C#/Db	G-Orange	G Pin # 4	00100	A #7	#4
#5	D#/Eb	G- Yellow	G Pin # 5	00101	A #6	#5
#6	F#/Gb	G- Green	G Pin # 6	00110	A #5	#6
#7	G#/Ab	G- Blue	G Pin # 7	00111	A #4	#7
#8	A#/Bb	G- Violet	G Pin # 8	01000	A #18	#8
#9	C#/Db	H- Black	H Pin # 1	01001	A #17	#9
#10	D#/Eb	H- Brown	H Pin # 2	01010	A #20	#10
#11	F#/Gb	H- Red	H Pin # 3	01011	A #19	#11
#12	G#/Ab	H- Orang	H Pin # 4	01100	A #14	#12
#13	A#/Bb	H- Grey	H Pin # 9	01101	A #13	#13
14 C	C#/Db	H- Green	H Pin # 6	01110	A #16	#14
#15	D#/Eb	H- Blue	H Pin # 7	01111	A #15	#15
#16	F#/Gb	H- Violet	H Pin # 8	10000	B #11	#16
#17	G#/Ab	I- Black	I Pin # 1	10001	B #9	#17
#18	A#/Bb	I- Brown	I Pin # 2	10010	B #10	#18
#19	C#/Db	I- Red	I Pin # 3	10011	B #8	#19
#20	D#/Eb	I- Orang	I Pin # 4	10100	B #7	#20
#21	F#/Gb	I- Yellow	I Pin # 5	10101	B #6	#21
#22	G#/Ab	I- Green	I Pin # 6	10110	B #5	#22
#23	A#/Bb	I- Blue	I Pin # 7	10111	B #4	#23
#24	C#/Db	I- Violet	I Pin # 8	11000	B #18	#24
#25	D#/Eb	J- Black	J Pin # 1	11001	B #17	#25
#26	F#/Gb	J- Brown	J Pin # 2	11010	B #20	#26
#27	G#/Ab	J- Red	J Pin # 3	11011	B #19	#27
#28	A#/Bb	J- Orang	J Pin # 4	11100	B #14	#28
#29	C#/Db	J- Yellow	J Pin # 5	11101	B #13	#29
#30	D#/Eb	J- Green	J Pin # 6	11110	B #16	#30
#31	F#/Gb	J- Violet	J Pin # 7	11111	B #15	#31

Fig 7.2 – Master Wiring Chart for the Black Keys

Starting with Fig 7.2 we see that the wiring of the black key solenoids to the middle pin of the Mosfets is exactly the same as for the white keys—solenoid to cable, then to the cable connector, then to the Mosfet. The difference comes about when we wire the gate of the Mosfet. The wire from the gate of the Mosfet does not go to the port directly, but instead goes to a decoder pin. The chart indicates the binary code used for the decoder and the decoder output pin that generates the output associated with each black key.

For example, we find that middle #C (C sharp or D flat) has a code of 01110 (16 octal or 14 decimal). The output pin of decoder A – pin 16 is wired to the gate of Mosfet 14. As with the white key connectors, we used left-over cable wire from the cable connectors to the Mosfet drains and solid #22 wire bundled in groups of 4 to go to the decoder outputs. The five decoder inputs come from Arduino ports 5, 6, 7, 8 and 9. Five solid, #22 wires bundled together fit tightly in the Mega's port connector to accomplish this part of the job. As we showed in Fig 5.5 and described in the text, output port 5 goes to pin 1 of the inverter and pin 23 of decoder A. Output ports 6, 7, 8, and 9 go to pins 22, 21, 3 and 2 of both decoders.

In the 60-key configuration, 25 black keys are activated rather than the 31 of a full-fledged keyboard. If 12 keys on each side of middle C are to be active, black key 1 and black keys 27 to 31 are not used. Simply cross them off the chart in Fig 7.2.

Master Wiring Chart for the White Keys (50-Key Config.)

White Key #	Note	Cable # Color	Connect # & Pin	Port #	Mosfet #
#6	C2	A- Green	A Pin 6	#22	#6
#7	D	A- Blue	A Pin 7	#23	#7
#8	E	A- Violet	A Pin 8	#24	#8
#9	F	B- Black	B Pin 1	#25	#9
#10	G	B- Brown	B Pin 2	#26	#10
#11	A	B- Red	B Pin 3	#27	#11
#12	B	B- Orang	B Pin 4	#28	#12
#13	C3	B- Yellow	B Pin 5	#29	#13
#14	D	B- Green	B Pin 6	#30	#14
#15	E	B- Blue	B Pin 7	#31	#15
#16	F	B- Violet	B Pin 8	#32	#16
#17	G	C- Black	C Pin 1	#33	#17
#18	A	C- Brown	C Pin 2	#34	#18
#19	B	C- Red	C Pin 3	#35	#19
#20	Mid C4	C- Orang	C Pin 4	#36	#20
#21	D	C- Yellow	C Pin 5	#37	#21
#22	E	C- Green	C Pin 6	#38	#22
#23	F	C- Blue	C Pin 7	#39	#23
#24	G	C- Violet	C Pin 8	#40	#24
#25	A	D- Black	D Pin 1	#41	#25
#26	B	D- Brown	D Pin 2	#42	#26
#27	C5	D- Red	D Pin 3	#43	#27
#28	D	D- Orang	D Pin 4	#44	#28
#29	E	D- Yellow	D Pin 5	#45	#29
#30	F	D- Green	D Pin 6	#46	#30
#31	G	D- Blue	D Pin 7	#47	#31
#32	A	D- Violet	D Pin 8	#48	#32
#33	B	E- Black	E Pin 1	#49	#33
#34	C6	E- Brown	E Pin 2	#50	#34
#35	D	E- Red	E Pin 3	#51	#35

Fig 7.3A – Master Wiring Chart White Keys (50-Key Config)

Master Wiring Chart for the Black Keys (50-Key Config.)

Key #	Note	Cable # Color	Connect # & Pin	Port #	Mosfet #
#5	D#/Eb	G- Yellow	G Pin # 5	#20	#5
#6	F#/Gb	G- Green	G Pin # 6	#1	#6
#7	G#/Ab	G- Blue	G Pin # 7	#2	#7
#8	A#/Bb	G- Violet	G Pin # 8	#3	#8
#9	C#/Db	H- Black	H Pin # 1	#4	#9
#10	D#/Eb	H- Brown	H Pin # 2	#5	#10
#11	F#/Gb	H- Red	H Pin # 3	#6	#11
#12	G#/Ab	H- Orang	H Pin # 4	#7	#12
#13	A#/Bb	H- Grey	H Pin # 9	#8	#13
14 C	C#/Db	H- Green	H Pin # 6	#9	#14
#15	D#/Eb	H- Blue	H Pin # 7	#10	#15
#16	F#/Gb	H- Violet	H Pin # 8	#11	#16
#17	G#/Ab	I- Black	I Pin # 1	#12	#17
#18	A#/Bb	I- Brown	I Pin # 2	#13	#18
#19	C#/Db	I- Red	I Pin # 3	#14	#19
#20	D#/Eb	I- Orang	I Pin # 4	#15	#20
#21	F#/Gb	I- Yellow	I Pin # 5	#16	#21
#22	G#/Ab	I- Green	I Pin # 6	#17	#22
#23	A#/Bb	I- Blue	I Pin # 7	#52	#23
#24	C#/Db	I- Violet	I Pin # 8	#53	#24

Fig 7.3B – Master Wiring Chart Black Keys (50-Key Config)

The 50-Key Configuration

Fig 7.3 A and B, seen above, show the wiring for the solenoids of the 50 keys. They relate closely to the other two Master charts. Fig 7.3A shows the wiring of the white keys and Fig 7.3B depicts the wiring of the black keys.

In Fig 7.3A we start with white key #6 and end with white key #35, for a total of 30 white keys. We show 5 cables and 5 connectors because this wiring chart is a subset of the 76-key configuration. Cable A and cable E can be combined into a single cable with a single connector since only 3 conductors are used in each cable. The wires to ports 22 to 51 are all plugged into the end double connector of the Arduino Mega. The Mosfets are arranged in a 4 by 8 array. The first Mosfet in this array is called Mosfet #5.

92

In Fig 7.3B we show the 20 black keys from 5 to 24 and solenoids 5 to 24 going to Mosfets 5 to 24. They are powered by ports 20, ports 1 to 17 and ports 52 to 53. The Mega's port 20 replaces port 0 which is reserved for coding musical pauses. Ports 52 and 53 replace ports 18 and 19 which are reserved for the sustain and low volume functions in all configurations. Ports 52 and 53 activate black keys 23 and 24. Port number 21 is a spare port.

It is important to note that here is considerable flexibility to the assignment of the keys on each side of middle C. In this 50-key configuration, we proposed assigning 14 white keys below middle C. That means that if you look at the sheet music of your favorite tune and, if there are no notes below the second ledger line, you win because all the notes can be played.

As far as the high notes go, you would be able to play the notes on two and one half ledger lines or the equivalent of 15 notes above middle C. If you activate the spare port on the high side you could play the notes on three ledger lines above middle C. It is for you to decide: the notes of a classic like Beethoven's "Fur Elise" go down to ledger line 1 and ½ below the bass staff and 3 ledger lines above the treble staff. So, with 51 keys would make it with one note to spare on the low side of middle C.

On the other hand, another of my favorites is Claude Debussy's "Claire de Lune." It goes a whopping 5 and 1/2 ledger lines above the treble staff. That translates to 21 notes above middle C (only 4 notes short of the 25 white keys available above middle C on the full Yamaha Keyboard). Unfortunately, the entire 76-key keyboard is needed to play this song.

Miscellaneous Wiring

The miscellaneous wiring described here is mostly the power wiring for the solenoids and for the decoder circuits as well as a recap of the sustain and volume control circuits discussed in Chapter 5. First, we must install the three IC sockets into which we will plug the inverter and the two decoders on the breadboard as shown on the diagram for the appropriate configuration. All the wiring to the IC's will be done to the pins of these IC sockets. Some of these wiring descriptions are necessarily similar to the descriptions of the electronic circuits in Chapter 5 but a little repetition won't hurt.

The 12 volt Power Circuit

The only power source needed for this project is a 12-volt power supply. It will be used to operate the solenoids and to power the Arduino Mega which, in turn will generate the +5 volt needed to power the IC logic (the inverter and the two decoders). The source of the 12-volt supply is the 120-volt wall socket. A 12-volt power supply similar to the ones used for PC's is used here to provide the DC power. The one that I have been using is rated at 3.0 amps which more than adequate, but be aware of the warning for this item (12) in Chapter 8. The output of the power supply comes out of a 2.5 mm coax plug. A matching receptacle is mounted at the top of the left-hand breadboard. From the receptacle, the 12-volt circuit goes to an on/off switch with a red LED. It is wise to turn off the 12-volt supply when the USB cable (with its own 5-volt supply) is plugged into the Mega to avoid two different voltage sources to the Arduino.

From the on/off switch, the 12-volt supply goes to three places. First, to 4 gray wires in the solenoid cables to bring power to one of the two solenoid wires. These 4 gray wires are soldered to the #14 bus wire mounted on the wooden crossbar to power all of the solenoids.

Second, to all the Mosfet diodes. And third, to the plug that powers the Arduino Mega when the USB cable is not connected. This last connection has two 10-ohm, 2-watt resistors wired in series in order to reduce the voltage to the Mega's voltage regulator (it gets very hot at 12 volts even though it is rated for that voltage). Using a different color wire for all the 12-volt runs is a good idea. The size of the wire is not critical but #24 stranded is ideal.

The 2.5 mm jack (receptacle) for the 12-volt power plug is mounted on the breadboard. Even mounted on a circuit board with solder through holes it has a flimsy mounting attachment. I have had problems (cold solder joints) after the plug has been inserted in the jack a few times. I strongly recommend that in addition to soldering the terminals of the jack on the breadboard, an additional bracket is made to hold it more securely. I have also used a #22 solid wire reinforcement which starts at the bottom of the breadboard, then wraps around the body of the jack and threads back through the breadboard with the ends of the leads twisted together. Soldering the wire to the "o" pads of the breadboard and soldering the twisted leads so that they won't unravel makes a stronger tie to the board. Ultimately, the 2.5 mm receptacle mounted on an angle bracket as shown in the photos makes an even better installation.

The 5 volt Power Circuit

The 5-volt power is used only for the computer IC components namely the two decoders and the inverter. It originates from the Arduino Mega's output connector marked +5, next to the two ground connections. Usually black or red wire is used. Since the runs are so short, solid #22 wire is acceptable here. Make sure you have a tight fit in the Arduino socket. From the Mega output pin, the wiring goes to the two #24 pins of the two MC14514 decoders and the #14 pin of the 7004 inverter.

The Ground Circuit

The ground wires are all tied together to form a single ground. Solid black wire (#24) is used to make most ground connections. One exception is where the wire is connected to the ground terminal of the Mega. A tight fit is needed here so use a #22 wire (tinned). The ground wire also connects to the ground connection at the 12-volt receptacle and to the source pin (right-hand pin) of each Mosfet via the ground busses.

Input Wiring to the Inverter and the Decoders

The input wiring to the inverter and decoders A and B is shown on the schematic diagram Fig 5.5. Not to worry, this is the only schematic diagram in the book! Note that 5K resistors to ground were added to each port to avoid floating ports when the Master Reset switch of the Mega is activated.

The output wiring of the decoders is shown on the Master Chart for the black keys of the 60- and 76-key configurations as well as on the schematic. At first blush the diagram may seem overwhelming, but as we break it down to its components, it becomes quite simple.

First, we will power the three IC components by wiring pin 14 of the inverter and pin 24 of each decoder to +5 volts. + 5 volts also goes to pin 1 of each decoder to keep the "Strobe" function energized (in this application it is not needed). Ground can be then be wired to pin 7 of the inverter and to pin 12 of each of the decoders to complete the power wiring.

I like to highlight the wires on the schematic after they have been installed to make sure that they all get wired in. Number 24 solid colored wire is the easiest to use. I use black for ground, red for +5 volts and white for the signal connections such as the ones going from the inverter to the decoder. When there are numerous signal wires in a close space, multi-colored wires made into a cable of 4 wires can be used to make it easy to check the wiring job. Such is the case when wiring the black keys going from the decoders to the Mosfets according to the Master Chart for the black keys (60- and 76-key configurations).

The Sustain and Volume Control Circuits

The relay shown in the diagram for the sustain circuit (Fig 5.2) turns on the sustain function. It is soldered in place at the top of the left breadboard. One side of its coil is connected to + 12 volts (like the solenoids) and the other side goes to the drain of a Mosfet, the same way as the solenoids. The Mosfet driving the relay can be located anywhere: it can be a spare location in the arrays or near the relay at the top of the left breadboard. The output port designated to activate sustain is always port 18. It will be assigned when the Robo sketch is described.

The wiring of the volume control contacts (see Fig 5.3) has been described and is located within the Yamaha. As with the sustain circuit, the coil is driven by a Mosfet which can be a spare located either in the solenoid arrays or at the top of the left board. The +12 volt and the return wire from the relay coil have to be routed to the inside of the Yamaha through a plug and jack mounted in the back of the Yamaha near the sustain jack. I suggested using a 3.5 mm plug and jack to distinguish it from the ¼ inch jacks used for the earphones and the sustain circuits. The output port designated to activate the volume control relay is always port 19. It will be assigned and described with the Robo sketch.

Soldering the Components in Place

I understand the perils of using connectors. Contacts and connectors are by far the greatest source of problems in electronic and computer circuits. Nevertheless, I recommend using IC sockets for the inverter and the two decoders IC's. These sockets are soldered to the breadboard and then the IC's are plugged into the sockets. The alternative is to solder the components into the breadboard directly. The problem with this method is that it is extremely difficult to remove a component without destroying the breadboard. In addition there is a possibility of damaging the component with too much heat when it is installed. These are good reasons for using IC sockets but be aware that they are rather flimsy—don't use too much heat to install them or the plastic will melt.

A picture being worth a thousand words, this last photo of Part 1 shows the top view of the breadboards populated with their components as well as the wiring of the cables. It is a duplicate of Photo 2.7 with the main components labeled.

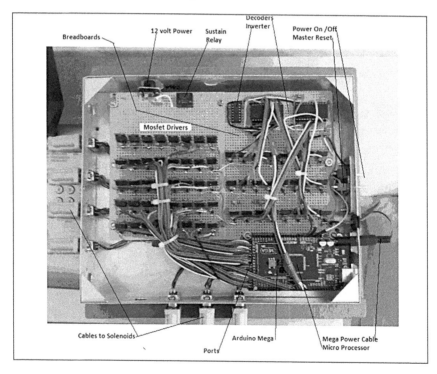

Photo 7.1 – Top View of the Control Box Components

Summary of Chapter 7

The complete job of wiring the control box was described using wiring charts showing the point to point wiring of the 76 solenoid coils to the Mosfet switches that energize them. The wiring of the Mosfet gates to the Arduino ports was also discussed. All three configurations were included.

Miscellaneous wiring which includes the volume control, the sustain circuit and the +12-volt and +5-volt power wiring was also described.

Chapter 8 will review the parts and components to be ordered as well as to provide some tips for their use. The amount of time needed to complete the tasks of populating the control box and doing the wiring will be estimated.

CHAPTER 8

Lists of Parts and Material

Building Material

The following list of parts and material will more or less follow the way we constructed the player piano. We will start with the construction material and continue to the electronics and the computer parts. Assembling and ordering parts sometimes require special discussions and instructions that we will provide along the way.

Construction Material

1. Pine board either 1x4 or 1x6, six feet long. #2 quality is OK as long as a 2 inch by 48 inch section which is straight and without twists or knots can be cut out. Home Depot or equivalent. $5

2. Two aluminum bars, 1/8 thick, 1.5 inch by 48 inch, $11 each at Home Depot. $22 total

3. Aluminum control box 8x10x2 inch. I paid $28 for mine at "U-Do- It-Electronics" which seems excessive. You might prefer shopping around to see if you can get a better deal.

4. 200 each M-3 stainless steel flat head screws 6mm long to mount the solenoids on the aluminum bars. Grainger part # HN4B00300-100. About $10

5. 100 each M3 brass nuts to mount the foot on the solenoid shaft. Grainger part number HN4B00300-100P1. About $6

6. Buttons or the equivalent: .060 in brass gasket material to make the foot. Jo-Ann's Fabric. Twenty 5/8 in buttons for $1. *See Chapter 3*

7. Miscellaneous wood screws and miscellaneous rubber grommets. Ace Hardware has better selections than Home Depot. $3

8. ¼ in threaded rod, 12 inches long, and 5/16 in threaded rod, 6 inches long; lock nuts and acorn nuts to attach the cross bar and the sound absorbing cover. $3

9. Sound absorbing cover. I had planned to use a heavy wood like oak (another hardwood would be equally good). I found a 4 foot piece of 1x10 oak ($12) which I ripped in 3 pieces. I think that an alternate and better selection turned out to be 3/8 inch chair rail material at Home Depot. Seven feet for approximately $15.

10. 25 foot rolls of wire.

    To connect from the Arduino ports to the Mosfets, use #22 solid (tinned) for a tight fit in the port connector. Buy 25 foot rolls of brown, yellow, orange and green. "All Electronics" cat # 22BR-25S, 22YL-25S, 22OR-25S, 22GN-25S. About $10

    To connect the cable connectors to the Mosfets, use left-over cable wire that has been stripped from the solenoid cables.

    For the power wires to the +5 volt use red #24 stranded; for to the +12 volt, use white #24 stranded. "All Electronics" cat # 24RD-25, 24WT-25. About $5

    For all other miscellaneous wiring jobs use black #24 solid wire or some of the left-over stranded wire. "All Electronics" cat # 24BK-25S. About $3

Tools

For the most part, no special tools are needed besides normal hand tools that do-it-yourselves have. A small drill press is a big plus to drill holes at 90 degree angles, but with great care a hand drill will do. An electric grinder and a vice are always useful. Miscellaneous drill bits and fine rat tail files will be needed.

A soldering iron and solder will be needed. Do not exceed 25 watts and use the thinnest solder wire (.022) available with rosin core. I like the lead based solder because it melts at a lower temperature. Additional flux will be needed to keep the soldering tips tinned and to solder to surfaces like the brass gasket material. (Radio Shack or electronics shops; also online). Always use as little solder as possible!

If you do not have one, buy an inexpensive multi-meter such as "All Electronics" DVM-810 for $8. It will come in handy to check for continuity and the value of the components.

Electronic and Computer Parts

The big expense in this list is the cost of the solenoids. 50 to 76 are needed and in view of the failures that I have had, I would add 10% for spares. One problem that I had that can easily be avoided is by being careful with the coil leads. I had a number of open circuits which could have been caused by pulling too hard on the leads when cutting or stripping the wires. Autopsies of these parts revealed open circuits at the coil.

1. To find the solenoids online, search using the term "solenoid JF-0730" It works on Ebay, Amazon and Alibaba (AliExpress). As of this writing, the best price on Ebay and Amazon is $6.79

with an upward range to $12. Dealing with AliExpress is a chore but it is worth it. When I bought a batch of 30 in November. 2014, they cost $3.03 including shipping. Today, I found the best price in lots of 10 at $2.11 (not including shipping).

It is a baffling system! How they can sell the same $3 unit for $7 to $12 boggles the mind! There is a way to have AliExpress get quotes online at "Stores" such as Store 1870168 or 1724883 or Chinese Wholesale Market or Electrical Kingdom. I have not done much shopping that way; back in 2014, Steve did it for me.

Watch out for shipping costs, as they vary greatly from China. Make sure to specify the right voltage, these solenoids come in 6, 12 and 24 volt versions. My only experience with returns from AliExpress is that, after a year, I am still waiting for an answer about my complaint regarding defective solenoids. Also, allow 2 to 3 weeks for delivery.

I would order the 10 units at $2.11 each and check them out before ordering anymore. As far as I can tell they are the right solenoids.

2. Arduino Mega 2560. You should be able to find it on Ebay for about $13. Buy a spare.

3. Two breadboards 4.5 x 6.25 in from Radio Shack. 2200 holes each. Keep the copper lands on the bottom. Re-drill and enlarge the mounting holes.

4. The IFR-520 Mosfets and the next 3 components make up one driver circuit. 50 to 76 of each are needed. Available from Ebay or from China. Approximately $.75 for each driver circuit.

5. 7404 Inverter. Ebay $1.

6. MC 14514 Decoder. Ebay $10 for two.

7. 150 ohm, ½ watt and 10,000 ohm, ¼ watt resistors. About $4 per lot of 100 at "All Electronics."

8. 1N4003 or 1N4004 diodes. About $6 for a lot of 100 at "All Electronics."

9. IC sockets (in which to plug the inverter and the decoder IC's). One 14 pins (ICS-14); two each 24 pins (ICS-24) Make sure they have the correct width. $1 at "All Electronics."

10. Six Extension cables, 6 feet, DB-9 connectors (CB-397) "All Electronics" $24 for 6 cables.

11. Connectors (solder style). Seven each DB-9P (male - plug) and 5 each DB-9S (female - socket). "All Electronics," about $5.

12. 12-volt power supply CAT # PS-123U "All Electronics," $8. Due to the light duty cycle of the 12 volt power supply, a 2.5 to 3 Amp rating is more than adequate for this power supply but be aware that many of these devices have an over-current circuit which turns off the device when the current rating is exceeded. It happened to me when playing chords requiring 4 solenoids to operate simultaneously. A larger power supply is the only solution.

13. Power jack to match power supply above. DCJ-25. Panel mount. "All Electronics," $2

14. On/Off switch for the 12-volt source. Cat # MTS-4PC. "All Electronics," $1

15. Master reset switch. To reset the computer. Momentary in one direction. "All Electronics" Cat # MTS-69, $1.

16. 3.5mm jack and plug for the volume control circuit. SMJ-2 and PMP. "All Electronics," $2

17. ¼ in plug for the sustain circuit. Cat # MPH-11. "All Electronics," $2.

18. 12-volt relays for the sustain and volume control circuits. Both need normally closed contacts when they are de-energized (NC). Sustain circuit: RLY-461; volume control circuit: RLY-622. "All Electronics," about $4.

Building Time for the Project

The construction of the wooden crossbar and the drilling and mounting of the aluminum bars is probably a three-day job.

The cables and connectors will probably take about two hours each.

I would allow a couple of hours per solenoid to modify, mount and wire them.

Building the control box should take about 8 hours

I know that it sounds excessive, but I estimate spending 10 minutes per wire to measure, strip, and solder it in place. There are probably 300 wires.

I would estimate spending half an hour per Mosfet driver with its 3 components to be soldered in place.

Plan on spending four hours each for both the sustain and volume control circuits.

The power circuits will probably take four hours.

The estimates above add up to approximately 250 hours. That may seem like a lot, but as a hobby that you spend 10-12 hours per week on, you'll be enjoying your very own player piano in just a few months.

Coding the Music

I have not done any serious coding of the sheet music. The amount of time depends greatly on the music that you chose to code. Until you get proficient, plan on spending 2 to 3 hours per page of sheet music (about a minute's worth of music). This is a job where two people can progress much faster than one person who has to view the sheet music, the translation charts and the Robo sketch for each note.

Total Cost for Various Configurations

It is not possible to give exact costs for each configuration because there can be some better values online than the prices at "All Electronics" where I procured most of the electronics. The cost of the solenoids alone can make a big difference. I think that there is enough detailed information above to do some serious shopping. Add $268 for the Yamaha keyboard described in this book.

•••

Totals for the 50-Key Configuration

Construction Material: $110

Electronic Parts and Components: $120

Solenoids: @ $3 $150   Grand Total: $380
•••

Totals for the 60-Key Configuration

Construction Material: $110

Electronic Parts and Components: $150

Solenoids: @ $3 $200   Grand Total: $460
•••

Totals for the 76-Key Configuration

Construction Material: $110

Electronic Parts and Components: $170

Solenoids: @ $3 $250   Grand Total: $530

PART 2

CHAPTER 9

Arduino IDE and the Mega

The Arduino Family of Computers

The Arduino phenomenon is about 10 years old. It started as a teaching device for students interested in computer science but it found many other enthusiastic users (approaching a million today) because of its low cost, ease of use and because it is an open source device. Open source means that the service is free and that there are no patents or copyrights to worry about. Anyone can use the hardware or the software as they see fit at no cost without the concern that they might be stealing someone's ideas. The only thing that cannot be used freely is the Arduino name.

There is an interesting origin story to the name Arduino. It came from the name of a bar in the city of Ivrea, Italy (now part of the city of Turin) where the founders used to meet. The bar itself was named after Arduin of Ivrea who was the king of Italy from 1002 to 1014. A subsequent dispute over the registration of the name caused the Arduino company to change the name of all Arduino products sold outside of the US to Genuino.

If you want more information about it, the Arduino web site, Wikipedia and numerous books have much more to say about this exciting company, its products and its rapid rise in popularity.

Arduino Computers

The Arduino web site tells us that there are 17 "official" Arduino computers available. That includes the Lillypad which is actually a wearable computer. About 15 older models are considered obsolete and have been retired but they may very well be on computer store shelves somewhere.

There are many clones on the market, but the real thing is inexpensive, reliable and of very high quality, so we will stick to the official brand. This is the third project that I have worked on using Arduino boards (I used the Uno for the other projects). The rugged reliability impressed me most. When doing research and development work, the oscilloscope is used constantly. In my hands, scope probes are weapons of electronic destruction. Flimsy circuits would not last long, but I can report that I have only burned out two Uno's and one Mega.

Selecting the Mega 2560 for this project was easy. We needed as many ports as possible to drive all those piano keys. Only two computers had 54 ports (the other computer, which is extremely fast, is mainly used for graphic applications). Simon Monk's book has a picture of the Mega 2560 and mentions that the flash memory has 128 kilobytes of storage (that's where the songs are stored, so it is an important specification). This information is not correct—I can vouch for the fact that there are 256 Kilobytes (KBs) of storage in the Mega 2560 which is sufficient for 2 hours' worth of music.

Arduino Shields

In addition to the good selection of computers, there is a large and varied collection of Arduino shields available (probably in the hundreds). Shields are PC boards (such as our breadboards) that perform functions such as driving robot motors or connecting to the Internet. There is even a new shield for one of the latest in high tech innovations: 3D printing

The clever part of the Arduino shields is that they plug into the connectors mounted all around the Arduino computer board. Moreover, they can be stacked on top of one another for additional circuits. If there were such a thing as a player piano shield with, say, 25 solenoid drivers in each shield, we could stack two or three of them on the Mega board, attach the solenoid wires to them and the entire wiring job would be done. Maybe I'll design one someday!

The Mega 2560

Now that we have selected the Mega 2560, let us see what is on the board and what makes its microprocessor, the ATmega 1280 tick. Don't let the microprocessor's small size fool you. It is very powerful and enormously complex: the data sheets for this microprocessor total 407 pages of small print. An interesting aspect of this device is that it is preloaded with a simple program that turns on an LED as soon as the power is applied for the first time from the USB cable or from an outside source of power. The orange LED near digital output port #13 blinks so as to say "Hello World!" Atmel, an American company, has manufactured more than 500 million of these units.

Starting with the microprocessor (the square block in the middle of the board with about 30 pins on each side), we see from the block diagram below, that it has a CPU (central processing unit) encircled by 3 types of memory units: 256KB of flash memory, 8KB of RAM (random access memory) and 4KB of EEPROM.

The CPU performs the byte transfers as well as the arithmetic calculations needed to solve formulas. During these operations it uses the very fast RAM working memory to store data temporarily. The flash memory is where the sketches are stored. Each line of code (one for each note) is executed sequentially in order to activate the piano keys. Within the sketch, the music is coded so that the proper key (or keys when a chord is played) is played for an appropriate amount of time. Part of the flash memory (8 KB) is also used for the bootloader.

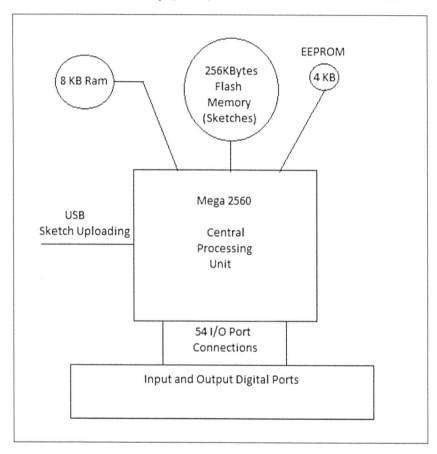

Fig 9.1 – Block Diagram of the ATmega 2560

The EEPROM memory, like the flash memory, is non-volatile: it does not lose data when the power is turned off. Compared to flash memory, it has the advantage of being able to be updated one byte at time and is used to store data that must not be lost when power is turned off or when the master reset switch is depressed.

Looking at a picture of the Mega 2560 in the same orientation as it is mounted in the control box (upside down!) we see two connectors on the right. The square connector at the bottom is for the USB cable. It is used to provide power to the board and to upload the sketches from the PC to the board. The top one is used to bring the 12-volt power to the board when the board is not connected to a PC with USB cable.

Going around the outside of the board in a counter-clockwise direction, there are three 8 pin connectors. The first one has the master reset pin plus voltage and ground pins, and the next two have 16 analog channels. At the end of the board, we find digital channels 22 to 53 in two rows of 18 pin connectors (the end pins are not used). Going around the bottom are two more 8 pin connectors and one with 10 pins for digital channels 0 to 21 plus ground pins. These are the connectors into which the shields plug in.

There are a number of other miscellaneous electronic components. The left orange button is the master reset switch which causes the microprocessor to start afresh and clear its memory. Nearby, there are numerous mini LEDS and some serial communication connectors.

The silver rectangular component between the two connectors on the right with "16,000" inscribed is the quartz crystal oscillator. It ticks away at 16 million ticks per second, and on each tick the microprocessor can perform one operation such as an addition. More complicated operations such as a multiplication, require several ticks but it is still lightning fast. The small cans are capacitors to smooth out the 3.3-volt and the 5.0-volt power that the built-in voltage regulators provide for additional circuits. Those are the main components on the board. Considering the power of the processor and the excellent quality of the board and its components, this is a world-class bargain at $13.

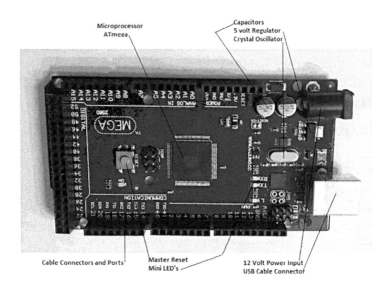

Microprocessor
ATmega

Capacitors
5 volt Regulator
Crystal Oscillator

Cable Connectors and Ports   Master Reset   12 Volt Power Input
Mini LED's   USB Cable Connector

Photo 9.1 – The Arduino Mega 2560

The Arduino IDE

When we refer to the Arduino IDE (Integrated Development Environment) we are talking about all the open source Arduino software that supports the development of all types of projects. The main uses of the IDE software that we download from the Arduino website are as follows.

1. Word processing. When we type either the sketch or the code for the music we use word processing software similar to Microsoft Word. With this software we are able to open new and old files and assign names to them so that they can be saved and retrieved. The word processor "File" button also controls the page set up and the printing functions.

2. Editor. This section of the word processor software makes it possible to "Copy" and "Paste" and, very importantly, to "Undo" errors. Copy and paste is very useful when coding music because music is so repetitive.

3. Compiler. After a sketch has been created, it is checked by the "verify" software which is part of the compiler. The words, the capital letters and the punctuation all have to be exactly correct or the verifier will reject it (and let you know about it!). Fortunately, the player piano sketch has been written for you so that this is not an issue. The compiler's main function is to translate the written words of the sketch into the 1's and 0's that computers understand. Any error in syntax discovered by the compiler is called out and must be corrected before anything else can proceed.

4. Drivers. They are needed so that your PC can communicate with the Arduino board using the USB channel. The installation of the drivers is not difficult; it is part of the installation of the Arduino IDE and it is explained step by step.

There are a number of other functions, operations and examples that are downloaded with the IDE which will be explained when we actually select and load songs into the Arduino board.

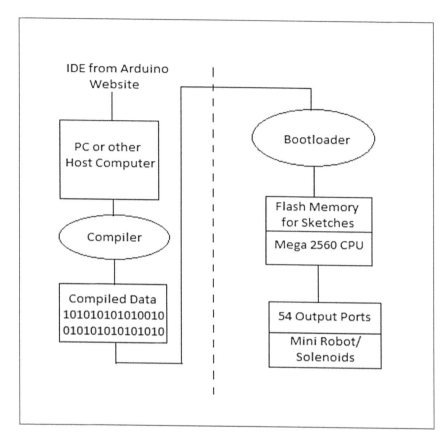

Fig 9.2 – Data Flow between PC and Arduino Board

The diagram shown above summarizes the flow of information. The data transfer from the Arduino website to the PC or another type of host computer is a one-time data transfer which brings all the support software into the host computer (your PC). Using mainly the word processor, a sketch is created; in our case, the sketch is called Robo. Within the sketch, a section is reserved for a line of code for each note of the music that we want to play.

After the music has been coded, the entire sketch is verified to make sure that there are no errors and is then, compiled. The compiling of the written words that we understand transforms these words into the 1's and 0's that the computer understands. This compiled data is then transferred and stored in the Mega's flash memory by the bootloader. All this activity takes place at the press of the upload button (right arrow). If the Mega's power is turned on, the music will start. It can be restarted at the beginning by pressing "Reset." To stop it, the power is turned off.

After the IDE has been downloaded and the Mega is connected to the PC, you can test it out by trying the following. Select the Arduino logo on your desktop. You will see a bare bones sketch with only the two commands that are needed for every sketch—"void setup" and "void loop". Go to "File" in the left-hand upper corner and click on "Examples." Select: "01 Basics," then click on the third item in the list, "Blink." You will now have a real sketch called Blink in front of you.

To upload it onto the Mega board, select the arrow pointing to the right. Assuming that the software drivers and the cable have been installed and that the correct microprocessor and communication channel (usually 3) have been selected, the sketch will be sent to the Mega board. The LED tied to channel 13 will blink once every second. If you want to play with the sketch just a little bit, you can change the 1000 millisecond delay to 100 milliseconds in both places and upload the sketch again. Now you will see the LED blink ten times faster.

Summary of Chapter 9

We took a look at the history of the Arduino company and analyzed why the Mega is the best choice for this project. Arduino supplies more than a dozen microprocessor boards which can be customized with dozens of shields for hundreds of applications. Their success is due to the high quality and low cost of their products in addition to the open source nature of their hardware and software.

The Arduino IDE makes it possible to program microprocessors such as the Mega 2560 from a PC or other host computers which run on a variety of operating systems. The programs (known as sketches in Arduino-talk) are then uploaded from the host PC to the Mega board. All necessary word processing, editing and compiler software is furnished in the IDE and it is all free.

Next, in Chapter 10, we will see how to activate the mini-robots so that they can play some tunes for us. You might have guessed that the very basic "Blink" program can also activate a mini-robot in which case the 1000 millisecond delay would generate a half note. We could then vary the length of the note by changing the delay.

CHAPTER 10

Activating the Mini-Robots

Computer Languages

B efore examining the very basic sketch "Blink," let us review the language that it is written in. Computer languages are somewhat like spoken and written languages such as English. Whereas there are thousands of words and definitions in English, there are only a few hundred in C or C++, the parents of the Arduino language which is used to program the sketches.

Our sketch "Robo," which will be used to play the music on the player piano has less than 50 different words and commands. To see the entire Arduino language, go to the Arduino IDE and look for the language reference under "Learning."

One of the simplest sketches in the Arduino library is "Blink." Using Blink as a foundation we will create "5 Sol," a diagnostic tool to check the operation and the noise level of a group of five solenoids. After this introductory exercise, we will describe Robo and explain how it is programmed to play music in Chapter 11. If you are interested in digging deeper into the programming of Arduino computers, Simon Monk's "Programming Arduino" is recommended.

A Simple Sketch

In Chapter 9, we mentioned that the simple sketch "Blink" could activate a mini-robot instead of an LED under the right circumstances.

I have copied and pasted Blink below (I changed the font size to make clear where the sketch starts and ends). To download the sketch from the Arduino IDE, click on the Arduino logo on your desktop and a new sketch will appear. Under File (in the top left-hand corner) click on "Examples," then on "01.Basic," then on "Blink." The sketch below will appear. My comments shown after the // in the sketch tell you how it works.

// the setup function runs once when you press reset or power the board

```
void setup()
{
  pinMode(13, OUTPUT);      // initialize digital pin 13 as an output
}
  void loop()               // the loop function runs over and over again
{
  digitalWrite(13, HIGH);   // turn the LED on (HIGH is the voltage level)
  delay(1000);              // wait for a second
  digitalWrite(13, LOW);    // turn the LED off by making the voltage LOW
  delay(1000);              // wait for a second
}
```

How "Blink" Works

Notice that the two required functions, the set-up function and the loop function, are present. Their parentheses are empty which means that there are no parameters associated with them. Right after each of these two functions, we see an open curly brace "{" and after the function has been specified, we see a closed curly brace "}". After "void loop," we also see an open curly brace and a closed curly brace after the four lines of code comprising the loop. These curly braces come in pairs and delineate the code to be executed before proceeding to the next instruction.

After the void setup, we find the command, pinMode(13, OUTPUT). PinMode refers to the pin of port 13 (one of the Mega's 54 ports) and it also sets the port to be an output port (as opposed to an input port). To activate a port you need to select it and also to tell the Arduino Mega whether it is used as an input or an output. This instruction will run once, and then the computer will proceed to the next line of code or instruction which is "void loop."

I replaced the #13 in three places in the sketch (port number and write command) with #36 which is the port number of the note "middle C." As expected, after uploading the sketch into a completely wired Control Box, the solenoid for middle C operated.

An extension of this exercise will be to create a short diagnostic sketch that we will call "5 Sol." Using "Blink" as a base, we will be able to test a group of five solenoids that we will mount on a leftover piece of aluminum bar. We want to test the solenoids at less than the normal 12 volts of source voltage and activate them for various time durations to measure the amount of noise that they produce. The results from such tests are successful when uniform readings are obtained from all solenoids as they are tested in groups of five. Label the solenoids and keep good records.

Notice an interesting aspect of this basic sketch. The // (double slash) is used to write comments about the code. When the sketch is verified/compiled, the compiler ignores everything on the line after the //. Sometimes, you may want to write a long comment or "comment out" several lines of code without doing it one line at a time. In that case, you can use /* at the beginning and */ at the end of the comment. The compiler will ignore everything between these notations. This comes in handy when you are looking for a typing error or if you have coded a song and something sounds wrong in the middle. By commenting out long sections before and after the questionable section, you can play just a few measures of the song repeatedly to locate the problem.

Testing a Group of Five Solenoids

We will energize the group of five solenoids two different ways. As we described in Chapter 3, before the control unit becomes operational, one lead from each solenoid is tied to the other four with a wire nut and connected to the +12-volt terminal of the battery (or a lower voltage to "marginal check" the operation of the solenoid). The other lead of the selected solenoid will go to battery ground through a switch (or the wire can just be ticked to the battery ground by hand). There is no danger of electrocution with 12 volts but avoid inadvertent short circuits that could ruin the battery.

After the control unit becomes operational, the solenoids can be checked with diagnostic sketch "5 Sol" which we describe in detail below. As before, we will test the five solenoids mounted on a short aluminum bar one at a time. The aluminum bar is mounted on the wooden crossbar with rubber grommets for noise suppression. One wire from each of the solenoids is connected with the other four and they are labeled +. For the noise test, + is tied to the +12 volts of the control box. For the marginal tests + is connected to a reduced voltage tap of a 12-volt battery. The − of the battery is connected to any ground pin in the control box. Of course, the control box 12-volt power supply is turned off during this marginal test.

The other wire from each of the solenoids is wired to a test cable (a left-over piece of cable with a male connector at one end) which will plug into connector C (see Fig 7.1, near the end of Chapter 7). We will be using middle C and the four notes above middle C (Keys 20 to 24 which are energized by ports 36 to 40). From Fig 7.1, we see that the wires that we will use in the test cable are colored orange, yellow, green, blue and violet. The short aluminum bar is mounted so that the left-hand solenoid activates Middle C. The orange wire connects to the second wire of this solenoid. The other cable wires are connected sequentially to the other four solenoids in the same manner.

Diagnostic Sketch to Operate 5 Solenoids

When the installation described above is completed, the "Blink" sketch should operate the Middle C solenoid if #13 is replaced by #36 in three places. The other four ports—37 to 40—and their solenoids are checked one at a time, in the same manner. All that needs to be done is to upload "Blink" each time with a different port number.

The next step is to create a simple sketch capable of activating a group of 5 solenoids sequentially and repeatedly to assess their operation and their noise characteristics. Using the Blink sketch as a base, three groups of code will be added or changed to activate this group of five solenoids. The names of the 5 solenoids will have to be defined in the setup section where we will also mention the names of the five ports to be used namely 36, 37, 38, 39 and 40. In the loop section, we will use a command that adds one (i ++) to the solenoid loop in order to activate the solenoids sequentially.

On my PC, I call the file containing the "5 Sol" diagnostic sketch "MPP 5 Solenoid Diagnostic." MPP stands for My Player Piano. I use this notation in front of every document or file relating to the player piano to make them easy to find among the rest of my files and documents.

The 5 Sol Diagnostic Sketch

Building on the Blink sketch, we will make the following changes to create the "5 Sol" diagnostic sketch. Refer to the flow diagram below in Figure 10.1. We have to expect this sketch to be longer and slightly more complex than Blink since we are activating 5 different solenoids sequentially.

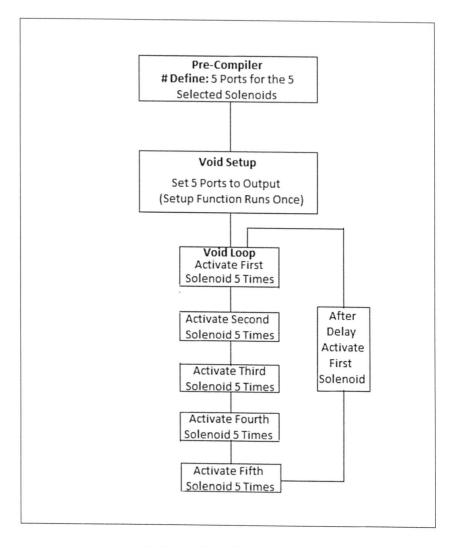

Fig 10.1 – Flow Chart for "5 Sol"

Each one of the solenoids will be activated for a given amount of time that we will call SOLTIME_DURATION. This is a good time to point out that, just as it is possible to describe a project using different words in the English language, it is equally possible to write a sketch in the Arduino language using different commands. For example, when we come to the point where we have to count to five we will use a command called "while," but we could have adjusted the code to use the command 'for" or the command "if." We used "while" because Robo uses both "while" and "if" and this is a good time to get accustomed to the meaning of these commands.

#Define

To specify which solenoids we want to operate and their time duration, the first 6 lines of the "5 Sol" sketch will use a directive called #define which allows a name to be associated with a value. Every time we write SOLPIN_1 in the sketch, the computer will know that we are talking about digital output port 36. We will therefore have the following 6 lines of code in the pre-compiler section of the sketch:

```
#define SOLPIN_1  36
#define SOLPIN_2  37
#define SOLPIN_3  38
#define SOLPIN_4  39
#define SOLPIN_5  40
#define SOLTIME_DURATION 500
```

We use capital letters with an underline between words because that is the way the names are coded in Robo. Usually the names are coded the same way as the functions. Their name starts with a lowercase letter and the next part of the name uses an uppercase letter without a space in between. For example, digitalWrite as seen in Blink. As long as we are consistent in our nomenclature, the compiler will be happy.

Using the #define directive saves memory space because it is not part of the compiler. It is run before the compiler and is therefore, known as a pre-compiler. But the main reason to define these words at the beginning of the sketch is that changing the port numbers is far more convenient. Consider the likely situation where the duration of the solenoid operation needs to be changed to, say, 200 milliseconds instead of 500. Without the #define SOLTIME_DURATION, the number 500 would have to be changed ten times in the sketch instead of just once.

Void Setup

Next, we have the first of the two required functions found in every sketch—void setup. The dreaded word "void" (which always throws me for a loop) needs an explanation. Most functions in C and Arduino return an answer after they are applied. For example, after solving an equation there is an answer, but setup and loop do not return an answer, they simply get something done. Consequently, Arduino must be told up front that an answer is not expected, hence the use of the word "void."

```
// the setup function runs once when you press reset or power the
board

void setup()
{                             // initialize digital pins 36 to 40 as outputs
  pinMode(36, OUTPUT);
  pinMode(37, OUTPUT);
  pinMode(38, OUTPUT);
  pinMode(39, OUTPUT);
  pinMode(40, OUTPUT);
}
```

As with Blink, the setup function in "5 Sol" (see flow chart in Fig 10.1) selects the desired port (in this case, the 5 desired ports) and sets them to output. Note that open and closed curly braces are placed at the start and end of this group of instructions. Because we used #define, the setup function allows the port numbers to be changed at the beginning of the program without making any changes to the main "loop" section of the program.

Void Loop

The void loop has 5 sections (one for each of the 5 solenoids) that are identical to the one described below. Each section starts with int i = 0;

```
void loop()           // the loop function runs over and over again forever
{
int i = 0;            //interger i starts at 0
while (i < 5)         //activate the same solenoid 5 times
{
digitalWrite(SOLPIN_1, HIGH);     // activate the solenoid
delay(SOLTIME_DURATION);          // wait for note duration
digitalWrite(SOLPIN_1, LOW);      // turn off the solenoid
delay(SOLTIME_DURATION);          // wait until the start of the next note
i ++;                             //run the loop again
}
```

Void loop() initiates a loop which activates the first of the five solenoids. The loop will be activated five times and after a ten-millisecond delay (which can be adjusted) the next solenoid will be selected and activated. The parentheses are empty, meaning that there are no parameters. A curly brace is opened after "loop" and will not be closed until the end of the loop after all 25 solenoid operations (5 solenoids operated 5 times each) have taken place.

The next step is to set integer i (this could be any letter or name but i is usually used for counting) to zero. The "while" command is used here to perform the five loops because it is used in Robo. As we have mentioned, other commands could be used to perform this routine. The expression in the parenthesis following "while" must remain true to stay in the loop. When it ceases being true (when i becomes 5), the sketch goes on to the next solenoid until it reaches the final curly brace (the other half of the curly brace pair which was opened after the loop command).

After i has been incremented five times (i ++ is a shortcut notation for "i +1") it is no longer less than five. Consequently, the program skips by the curly brace and moves on to the next solenoid loop which starts with a delay. We used a 10 millisecond delay which is not noticeable but it can be increased to several seconds to allow time to make notes or for some other reason. The next "while" command has "i < 10" in its parenthesis which will allow i to be incremented 5 more times for the operation of the next solenoid (SOLTIME_2).

When i reaches 10 the program skips past the next curly brace and moves down the loop which activates the third solenoid. This same sequence of events will continue through solenoids four and five until i reaches 25. At this point, instead of a short 10-millisecond delay, the delay has been increased to three seconds to indicate that a whole cycle of 25 operations for the 5 solenoids has been completed. After this three-second delay, the second curly brace is reached and it directs the program back to the beginning of the loop where it starts over. Note that the flow diagram shows the line from the fifth box going to the "void" box. The complete "5 Sol" sketch is shown on the following pages.

The 5 Sol Sketch

```
#define SOLPIN_1 36              //define the solenoid output ports
#define SOLPIN_2 37
#define SOLPIN_3 38
#define SOLPIN_4 39
#define SOLPIN_5 40
#define SOLTIME_DURATION 500     //define the duration of the operation
void setup()                     // the setup function runs once when
{                                //you press reset or power the board
  pinMode(SOLPIN_1, OUTPUT);     //initialize output ports 36,37,38,38,40
  pinMode(SOLPIN_2, OUTPUT);
  pinMode(SOLPIN_3, OUTPUT);
  pinMode(SOLPIN_4, OUTPUT);
  pinMode(SOLPIN_5, OUTPUT);
}
  void loop()                    //the loop function runs over and over
{
  int i = 0;
  while (i < 5)
{
  digitalWrite(SOLPIN_1, HIGH);  //turn the solenoid on
  delay(SOLTIME_DURATION);       //wait for the delay period
  digitalWrite(SOLPIN_1, LOW);   //turn the solenoid off
  delay(SOLTIME_DURATION);       //wait for the delay period
  i ++;                          //add one to the count
}
  delay (10);
  while (i < 10)
{
  digitalWrite(SOLPIN_2, HIGH);  //turn on solenoid 2
  delay(SOLTIME_DURATION);
  digitalWrite(SOLPIN_2, LOW);
  delay(SOLTIME_DURATION);
  i++;
}
  delay (10);
  while (i < 15)
{
  digitalWrite(SOLPIN_3, HIGH);  //turn on solenoid 3
```

```
delay(SOLTIME_DURATION);
digitalWrite(SOLPIN_3, LOW);
delay(SOLTIME_DURATION);
i ++;
}
delay (10);
while (i < 20)
{
digitalWrite(SOLPIN_4, HIGH);        //turn on solenoid 4
delay(SOLTIME_DURATION);
digitalWrite(SOLPIN_4, LOW);
delay(SOLTIME_DURATION);

i ++;
}
delay (10);
while (i < 25)
{
digitalWrite(SOLPIN_5, HIGH);        //turn on solenoid 5

delay(SOLTIME_DURATION);
digitalWrite(SOLPIN_5, LOW);
delay(SOLTIME_DURATION);
i ++;
}
delay (3000);
}                                    // start the 5 solenoid loop again
```

Setting up the "5 Sol" Sketch on your PC

Creating a file for the "5 Sol" sketch can be done by typing the sketch shown above in a new Arduino file (click on Arduino, File, New). First, type in the title (5 Sol) then the #defines. Notice that the void setup and the void loop commands are already there (I suppose that Arduino does not want you to forget these essential commands). As I mentioned before, there is a lot of repetition in the sketches. Instead of typing each line of code, it is much easier to type one line and copy/paste it on the next line and make the corrections needed for the new line. When you get to the four lines which select the solenoid and its duration, all four lines can be copied and pasted at once.

It easy to make a typing error or some other error that will cause the compiler to reject your efforts. Moreover, it is not easy to interpret the compiler's error messages. I find it good practice to compile/verify the code after a curly brace for the void commands is closed. That way you won't compound the difficult task of locating the errors by having more than one section to contend with at one time. My most common errors are leaving out a semicolon (the compiler gets equally upset if you put a semicolon where it is not needed) and not pairing up the curly braces properly.

Use of the 5 Sol Sketch

This sketch is most useful to make sure that all solenoids operate correctly and that the correct key is activated according to the port number that is selected by the software.

It is also a good way to compare the operation of the solenoids when the 12-volt supply is reduced (by using a battery with lower voltage taps as the 12-volt supply) as we did in Chapter 3. We need to make sure that there is consistent operating margin between the 12-volt supply voltage and the voltage at which the solenoids operate reliably. These marginal check tests are again conducted by reducing the 12-volt source in 1.5 volt steps to make sure that we have a measure of safety when we depress the keys. A successful test shows consistent results for all 5 solenoids around 7.5 to 9.0 volts.

Finally, it is an excellent vehicle to test the effect of the noise suppression that we added to the solenoids. The tests conducted in Chapter 3 should be repeated at this time under computer control using 5 Sol. They will quickly locate any solenoid in need of further noise reduction work.

Summary of Chapter 10

We quickly reviewed how programming languages work by down-loading the simple sketch "Blink" and explained how it works. Then, by changing the output port, we operated one of the solenoids mounted on the keyboard.

Using "Blink" as a base, we expanded this simple sketch so that it would repeatedly activate 5 solenoids. The new sketch is named "5 Sol." A flow chart showing the "#define," the "void setup" and the "void loop" functions was presented. Every line of code was de-scribed and the need for each command was explained. The code de-tailed here is intended to be used to check out 5 solenoids one at a time to assess their correct operation as well as the amount of noise that they produce. The code can be modified to select any group of five solenoids by selecting their output ports as well as the duration of their operation. A copy of "5 Sol" is included above. If this is all new to you, do not hesitate to read and re-read these instructions sev-eral times to become familiar with them.

Creating "5 Sol" to test the solenoids was an excellent exercise to get a feel for what is needed to create an Arduino sketch capable of playing notes. Obviously, playing music is more involved which in turn causes the Robo sketch to be more complicated. Fortunately, it has been written and tested for us. Now that we've gone through this introductory exercise, we will describe Robo and explain how it can be programmed to play music in the next chapter.

CHAPTER 11

The Song Playing "Robo"

"Robo" is the name we gave to the Arduino sketch (the software program) which plays the player piano's songs. It resides in the brain of the player piano's control box and activates the solenoids which in turn depress the piano keys. In order to perform this feat, it must be told eight characteristics about each note to be played. The music coder is the person who provides this data in the form of one line of code for each note. The data comes from the song's sheet music and is interpreted by the music coder. Some of the information must come from the music coder's musical ability. For example, the beat of the song is not usually provided in the sheet music. Additionally, the use of the volume and sustain pedals is also at the musician's discretion. The music coder should expect to have to do some trial and error when selecting the beat and simulating the operation of the pedals. We will show some techniques that make this exercise as painless as possible.

Comparing Robo to 5 Sol

Seeing that we just described the operation of 5 Sol sketch which also activates solenoids, let's look at the other functions needed to play music instead of simply operating our mini-robots.

- Implement the decoding and selection of the solenoids for the accidentals or black keys

- Activate the volume control port
- Activate the sustain port
- Devise a formula to combine the duration of the notes with the beat of the music and the duration of the solenoid operation
- Provide a programmable way to play cords

These additional functions (the last two being the difficult ones) are all implemented by executing the line of code that applies to the note to be played. Illustrated below in block form are the eight pieces of information that make up a line of code for each note.

An example of the coding for a white key and for a black key looks like this:

1	2	3	4	5	6	7	8
Select Ports (For B&W Keys)	Beat of the Song	Sustain Pedal	Low Volume Pedal	Note Duration	Solenoid Duration	Chords (multiple selection of Keys	Black or White Keys

{36, 0, 0, 0, 0, 0, BEAT_100, 0, 0, DURATION_FULL, SOLTIME_A, 0, WHITE_KEY},
{0, 1, 0, 1, 0, 0, BEAT_100, 0, 0, DURATION_EIGHTH, SOLTIME_B, 0, BLACK_KEY},

The meaning of each block of information which is separated by a comma is explained below. Photo 11.1 and Fig 11.1 are the references needed to select the appropriate port number.

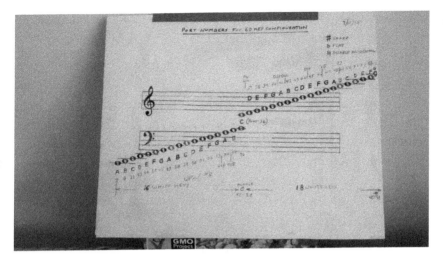

Photo 11.1 – Port Numbers for a 60-Key Configuration

Selecting a Port for a White or Black Key

{*36, 0, 0, 0, 0, 0*, BEAT_100, 0, 0, DURATION_FULL, SOLTIME_A, 0, *WHITE_KEY*},
{*0, 1, 0, 1, 0, 0*, BEAT_100, 0, 0, DURATION_EIGHTH, SOLTIME_B, 0, *BLACK_KEY*},

The examples above show blocks 1 and 8 in bold italics. They are combined to select the ports for the white and black keys (the naturals and the accidentals). As we have mentioned before, the port determines which key is to be depressed. Block 8 tells us whether we are dealing with a white or a black key. Before the first comma in the line of code, the port number of the white key is declared. If this line of code is for a black key, a "0" is typed where the white key port number would go. If a white key is being coded, its port number is typed in. The port number is obtained from the note chart (Fig 4.2 or Photo 11.1 above) by the music coder as he/she assigns a port number to the note. In the example above, the port number for note "middle

C" is 36. The music coder types in 36, followed by a comma and because it is not a black key, five zeros separated by commas.

If this were a black key, the music coder would put a zero (where the port number of a white key would go) followed by a comma after this first slot to indicate that it is not a white key. He would then obtain the port number of the black note in binary from the master wiring chart 7.2 or from the part which is reproduced in Fig 11.1. The music coder then inserts the binary ones and zeroes in the next five slots separated by commas. In the example above for black key #20, port number 24 (octal) was selected and converted to binary.

Before going on with the next block to be coded, it is important to understand the information found in Photo 11.1. It is a drawing of the notes and their port numbers for a 60-key configuration. Starting at middle C, we see that 16 keys can be activated below middle C and 18 can be activated above middle C. That comprises the 35 white keys with solenoids. This results in the ability to play a low E and a high G. These low and high notes reside on the third ledger lines below the bass staff and on the fourth ledger line above the treble staff. A quick look at the sheet music selected tells you whether all the notes are within the range of the playable notes. With such a wide range, it's unlikely that they would not be.

The port numbers for the black keys ("Fur Elise" has 8 of them) were added in octal next to the white port numbers. They can be added to a chart like this, or the port number can be determined each time by consulting a separate chart, such as Fig 11.1 which shows the sharp and flat notes associated with each white key. Photo 11.1 is difficult to read, but to the right of middle C is an octal 16. It means that the fourteenth black key is a C sharp with an octal port of 16 (01110 in binary).

Port Translator for the Black Keys			
Black Key #	Keyboard Note	Octal Port Number	Binary Port Number
#1	F#/Gb	1	00001
#2	G#/Ab	2	00010
#3	A#/Bb	3	00011
#4	C#/Db	4	00100
#5	D#/Eb	5	00101
#6	F#/Gb	6	00110
#7	G#/Ab	7	00111
#8	A#/Bb	10	01000
#9	C#/Db	11	01001
#10	D#/Eb	12	01010
#11	F#/Gb	13	01011
#12	G#/Ab	14	01100
#13	A#/Bb	15	01101
#14 Mid C	C#/Db	16	01110
#15	D#/Eb	17	01111
#16	F#/Gb	20	10000
#17	G#/Ab	21	10001
#18	A#/Bb	22	10010
#19	C#/Db	23	10011
#20	D#/Eb	24	10100
#21	F#/Gb	25	10101
#22	G#/Ab	26	10110
#23	A#/Bb	27	10111
#24	C#/Db	30	11000
#25	D#/Eb	31	11001
#26	F#/Gb	32	11010
#27	G#/Ab	33	11011
#28	A#/Bb	34	11100
#29	C#/Db	35	11101
#30	D#/Eb	36	11110
#31	F#/Gb	37	11111

Fig 11.1 – Binary Port #'s for the Black Keys

The fancy stand for the port number diagram pictured above was made from a cereal box. Being at eye level, a diagram like this is useful to translate the sheet music notes to port numbers. I recommend making a chart such as this to ease the job of determining the port numbers. Seeing that there are so few unique black notes used, I add them to the chart as they come up. They are usually repeated several more times in the song.

Box 2: the Beat of the Song

{36, 0, 0, 0, 0, 0, ***BEAT_100***, 0, 0, DURATION_FULL, SOLTIME_A, 0, WHITE_KEY},
{0, 1, 0, 1, 0, 0, ***BEAT_100***, 0, 0, DURATION_EIGHTH, SOLTIME_B, 0, BLACK_KEY},

The beat of the song to which your foot or hands keep in step, varies greatly between songs. When you buy the sheet music of a composer like Beethoven, don't expect a metronome value to tell you what the beat is. At the start of the music, all it might say is "Poco Moto." There is no hint as to what section of the song it applies to, so the music coder has considerable leeway in selecting the beat for the song. A virtuoso pianist playing a version of "Fur Elise" is recorded in the Yamaha keyboard. The beat varies between roughly 100 to 140 beats per minute. 110 BPMs would be a good starting point. Since the beat can be changed one note at a time, the music coder is capable of speeding up the beat or slowing the beat down at will.

We will see that the "#defines" are the definition of the many variables that we need to play a note. In Robo, they determine the beat and range between 60 and 300 beats per minute as determined by a metronome. The Robo software does not impose any limit on the duration of a beat so that the BEAT range could be expanded if need be. At the mid-point, "BEAT_120" is associated with 500. That simply means that at 120 beats per minute, the duration of each beat is

500 milliseconds (120 beats per minute equals 2 beats per second, therefore, each beat lasts 1/2 second or 500ms.). This number will be one of three factors that determine how long the solenoid remains energized when it is used to play a note in a song.

Boxes Three and Four

{36, 0, 0, 0, 0, 0, BEAT_100, *0, 0,* DURATION_FULL, SOLTIME_A, 0, WHITE_KEY},
{0, 1, 0, 1, 0, 0, BEAT_100, *0, 0,* DURATION_EIGHTH, SOLTIME_B, 0, BLACK_KEY},

These two boxes are easy. If the music coder desires to use the sustain feature or the low volume feature, he simply places a 1 in box three and/or box four. Sustain and/or low volume will become active starting with that note and stay active as long as the following notes have 1's in these boxes. These two features simulate the action of the left and right piano pedals. They are turned off when a 0 is detected in these positions. As with the other information in the note's line of code, commas are placed after the 1's or 0's.

Coding the Note Duration

{36, 0, 0, 0, 0, 0, BEAT_100, 0, 0, *DURATION_FULL,* SOLTIME_A, 0, WHITE_KEY},
{0, 1, 0, 1, 0, 0, BEAT_100, 0, 0, *DURATION_EIGHTH,* SOLTIME_B, 0, BLACK_KEY},

Looking at any sheet music, we see notes of different durations from full notes with open circles to sixteenth notes with the double tails. From our example, where the quarter note had the beat, we would expect the full note to last four times as long as the quarter note and the sixteenth note to last one quarter of the quarter note's duration. Using this information, Robo will determine that when the beat is

139

120 beats per minute, the quarter note should last 500ms, the full note should last 2 seconds while the sixteenth note should last 125ms. I say "should" last 500ms because these note durations are multiplied by one more factor the "SOLTIME," which is the amount of time that the solenoid is energized, as recorded in Box 6. For normal notes, this multiplier is set at 75%. So in our example the actual duration time of the solenoid closure will be 375 ms. Let's be clear, when the beat is 120 BPM, the note duration for a quarter note is 500ms—that is set in concrete. The next note will not start before the 500ms have elapsed. However, the solenoid duration may cause the key to be depressed for a shorter period of time. While normal (B) is 75% of beat, we will see that SOLTIME occasionally ranges from 25% to 100% of the beat in order to play chords correctly and/or to play notes whose duration is 50% longer than normal (when there is a dot next to the note).

Solenoid Duration – Box 6

{36, 0, 0, 0, 0, 0, BEAT_100, 0, 0, DURATION_FULL, *SOLTIME_A,* 0, WHITE_KEY},
{0, 1, 0, 1, 0, 0, BEAT_100, 0, 0, DURATION_EIGHTH, *SOLTIME_B,* 0, BLACK_KEY},

As we mentioned above, the solenoid duration can be set from 25% to 100% of the beat for various reasons. The normal setting is 75% of the beat. But occasionally, especially in classical pieces, a chord has to be played where, for example, one of two notes in the chord transforms itself into a third note before the chord ends. To provide the ability to play such a chord correctly, the duration of the solenoid time (SOLTIME) is divided in 25% segments. A normal B, equal to 75% of the beat, is used most of the time.

Playing Chords

{36, 0, 0, 0, 0, 0, BEAT_100, 0, 0, DURATION_FULL, SOLTIME_A, *0,* WHITE_KEY},
{0, 1, 0, 1, 0, 0, BEAT_100, 0, 0, DURATION_EIGHTH, SOLTIME_B, *0,* BLACK_KEY},

While coding the average piece of music is straightforward and easy to do once you get the hang of it and start remembering a few of the common port numbers, coding the chords takes some thinking. We will ease into it with "Saints" which has lots of chords, and later move into Beethoven's chords which are quite special. The example above has no chords, which is reflected in box 7 with a bold, italic 0.

Basically, what we do, is to write a line of code for the first note in the chord and call it "Start" in Box 7. Then, assuming that there are four notes in the chord, we write a second line of code for the second note in the chord and call it "Continue." We repeat this for the third note in the chord. For the last note, we write another line of code and call it "End." For a two-note chord there would only be a "Start" and an "End" in Box 7 of the two lines of code.

It does not matter which note is called note "one," since by the definition of a chord all notes are played simultaneously. To keep it simple, I call to top note on the scale "note one" and the bottom note on the scale, "note four." Since we only have five fingers on each hand, few chords are found with more than 4 notes! The Robo sketch will sort out these four lines of code and play all the notes at the same time, then move on to the next note. In Chapter 12, on coding the music, we will describe the more complicated chords that are found in classical pieces such as Beethoven's "Fur Elise." In the Robo sketch's interpretation of chords, the soltime value assigned to the "END" note applies to the entire chord.

141

Introductory Code for the Robo Sketch

Before we really get serious about coding music or describing the Robo sketch, we need to describe the range of choices that is available to the coder to specify the characteristics of each note as shown in the blocks of information described above. Note that the order in which the "#define" choices are listed does not have to correspond to the order in the line of code. The correct order will be set by the structure of the array as we will see below.

Beat of the Song

The "#defines" for the beats are shown below. Additional "#defines" can be added if necessary. When coding a song, I use the same beat number for an entire page for the first cut at coding the music. One example is BEAT_150, which is a fast beat whose note duration is 400 ms. I will then listen to the rendition and try a slower beat, say, BEAT_120. But I will use the following little trick: instead of going through the whole page of coding and replacing all the 150's with 120's, I will simply replace the 400 (in BEAT_150 400) with 500 and do a compile/upload. Like magic, Robo will change the beat of all the notes on the page of music and you will hear your song played at a slower beat. You can continue making changes to this "global" beat number until you find the perfect beat.

```
#define BEAT_60 999      //Number of ms for various beats
#define BEAT_70 857      // using a metronome's "beats per minute"
#define BEAT_80 750
#define BEAT_90 666
#define BEAT_100 600
#define BEAT_110 550
#define BEAT_120 500
#define BEAT_130 467
#define BEAT_140 433
```

```
#define BEAT_150 400
#define BEAT_160 375
#define BEAT_170 352
#define BEAT_180 333
#define BEAT_300 200        //Used for very short "Blip" notes
```

Duration of the Notes

What we are defining in this section is the duration of the notes from full notes to notes that last only one sixteenth the duration of a full note.

```
#define DURATION_FULL 1        //Defines the multiplier needed
#define DURATION_HALF 2        //to determine the length of the note
#define DURATION_QUARTER 3
#define DURATION_EIGHTH 4
#define DURATION_SIXTEENTH 5
```

```
static int beatMult [] = {0,16,8,4,2,1};
```

The numbers 1, 2, 3, 4, 5 are used to select a multiplier from 16 to 1 which will be used in the Robo formula to determine the duration of notes based on the beat of the song. When the quarter note has the beat, its time duration will be equal to the beat time listed in the #define number selected. A full note will last four times longer than the quarter note and a sixteenth note will last one quarter of its duration. The reason for using all integers instead of fractions is that the Mega microprocessor handles calculations using integers much better and faster than fractions.

The last line of the code above starting with "static" needs some explanation. The keyword "static" is used so that the variable (in this case "beatMult") will only be initiated the first time the function is called. It is then set in concrete and cannot be changed. The [] tells us that beatMult is in the form of an array instead of a single integer.

An array is used to contain a list of similar variables which can be accessed with a pointer to select their value depending on their position in the list. As we can see, the values in the array are within the curly braces and separated by commas. Robo will sort out this information to determine the correct duration of the notes.

Solenoid Activation

As we discussed above, the solenoids can be activated for 100% of the time as calculated for the note being coded or for a lesser amount of time namely, 75%, 50% or 25% of the time. This feature is necessary for some cords, notes with dots and certain very short notes ("blips") that are sometimes found in the sheet music. SOLTIME_B (the normal setting) would therefore reduce the 100% solenoid duration as calculated from the beat, to a duration of 75%.

```
#define SOLTIME_A 4    //Solenoid stays energized for 100% of the duration of the note
#define SOLTIME_B 3    //Solenoid stays energized for 75% of the duration of the note
#define SOLTIME_C 2    //Solenoid stays energized for 50% of the duration of the note
#define SOLTIME_D 1    //Solenoid stays energized for 25% of the duration of the note
```

Activating the Sustain and Low Volume Features

Activating the sustain feature or a lower volume feature (a sound level called "piano," incidentally) simply involves selecting ports 18 and 19 and keeping these ports active (high) for as long as the music coder desires. Sustain is associated with port 18 and volume control is associated with port 19. SUSTAIN_ON is defined as a 1 while SUSTAIN_OFF is defined as a 0. VOLUME_LOW is defined as a 1 and VOLUME_HIGH is defined as a 0. We will see later that the Robo sketch will interpret these values by turning ports 18 and 19 on and off. The #define code is shown below.

```
#define SUSTAIN_ON 1
#define SUSTAIN_OFF 0

#define VOLUME_LOW 1
#define VOLUME_FULL 0
```

Activating the Chord Software

To play chords it is necessary to select several notes and play them simultaneously. This is done by replacing the 0 which would be in box 7 for a "non-chord" note. The first note of a chord is called "CHORD_START." If the chord has two notes the next note is called "CHORD_END" in box 7. If there are more than two notes the second and the following notes are called "CHORD_CONTINUE." The sequence is, Start, Continue, End, with the possibility of more than one "Continue." The code for the chord #defines is shown below.

```
#define CHORD_START 1
#define CHORD_CONTINUE 2
#define CHORD_END 3
```

Defining the Keys and Ports

The ports are last to be defined although they appear first in the line of code. They will be decoded to activate the solenoids which, in turn, depress the keys. First, we have to know if it is a white or a black key. The answer, in box 8, is used to select the appropriate groups of ports. For the white keys, the ports are 0 to 4, 10 to 17 and 20 to 53 to activate the 45 ports of a 76-key configuration. As we have discussed, the ports for the black keys are coded so that only 5 ports, 5 to 9 are needed to select the 31 black keys.

The ports are broken down in odd groups for two reasons. First, we want approximately the same number of keys on each side of middle C in the reduced key configurations. Second, the groups are arranged so that they can easily be commented out of the Robo code when they are not needed. With this design we can readily implement 50-key and 60-key configurations as well as the full 76-key configurations according to the wiring charts Figs 7.1, 7.2 and Figs 7.3 A and B.

```
#define WHITE_KEY 0
#define BLACK_KEY 1

#define START_FIRST_KEY 0
#define END_FIRST_KEY 4

#define START_BLACK_KEY 5
#define END_BLACK_KEY 9

#define START_CONFIG_KEY 10
#define END_CONFIG_KEY 17

#define START_WHITE_KEY 20
#define END_WHITE_KEY 53


#define SONG_END 255
```

The last line tells us that while Robo is cycling (looping) through the notes, if it runs into a port 255 (which does not exist) it means that it has reached the end of the song. At this point, Robo will restart playing the song or move to the first note of the next song.

Structuring the Note

Now that we know what all our choices are, we will structure them in the order required by the line of code used for each note and, at the same time, we will assign the most efficient number of bits to the variables in the structure.

```
struct myNote
{
    byte Port;
    byte blackStateP5: 1;
    byte blackStateP6: 1;
    byte blackStateP7: 1;
    byte blackStateP8: 1;
    byte blackStateP9: 1;
    int  Beat;
    byte Sustain :   2;
    byte Volume :    2;
    byte Duration:   4;
    byte Soltime:    4;
    byte Chord :     4;
    byte BlackKey :  4;

} Note;
struct myNote Elise[] = {
```

The structure above is similar to an array in that it contains bits of information that can be assessed by their location in the structure with a pointer. The information can be more varied than the integers that we had in the DURATION array. A useful feature of this structure is that each bit of information can be assigned the minimum number of bits needed to define it.

This structure is named "myNote" and declared using the expression: struct myNote. Curly braces open and close the structure. Within the curly braces we find all the items that are needed to define a note. We have talked many times about the eight pieces of information needed to define a note. The reason that there are 13 lines of code in the structure is that defining a port requires 6 pieces of information, one for the white keys and 5 for the black keys whose port selection is coded.

This first "struct" declaration is used to pack the data efficiently. Port and beat require a byte (or more) to specify their value but the rest of the information does not require an entire byte to specify its value. Notice that after the colon there is a number from 1 to 7. It indicates the number of bits required to specify the function. For example, sustain and low volume require two bits each. This is important because it makes the coding of the notes more efficient. Therefore, it uses less memory and provides more room to upload more notes or songs at one time.

After closing this structure we open a new structure that will contain all the note data to play a song. In this case, it will be Beethoven's "Elise". The declaration is written as follows: "struct myNote Elise[] =". We now open a curly brace and the music coder can start coding each note with the eight bits of information needed for each note.

"struct" is used in C to define a variable in a way similar to an array. Strangely, while "struct" is not mentioned in Simon Monk's book or in the definition of terms in the Arduino IDE language reference, it compiles perfectly well. This is not a fluke. If an error is made while coding, the compiler is quick to pick it up and let you know about it.

This discussion concludes the preliminaries for the coding of the music which we will continue to describe in the next two chapters. Think about this section as being the foreplay for the music.

Summary of Chapter 11

We are now in the process of describing the sketch called Robo which activates the keys to play piano music. Chapter 11 describes the preliminary information needed by Robo and sets up the structure in which the note data will be coded. Chapters 12 and 13 will show how to code the notes and Chapter 14 will describe how the Robo sketch works. While some readers may find this discussion very interesting, it is by no means essential to produce music from the keyboard. Correctly coding the notes found in the sheet music is far more important than knowing how Robo works.

Using a box format, we described all the information needed to play a note: from selecting the beat of the music to deciding whether we are dealing with a white or black key. We then described the eight groups of "#define" which select the correct solenoids and affect the amount of time that these mini-robots are energized. Finally, we set up the structure of the line of code used for each note and we selected a method of packing the data efficiently.

CHAPTER 12

Coding a Song

We have reached the point where a song presented in sheet music form can be translated into the language that the Arduino Mega understands. The attributes of the notes shown in the sheet music will be transformed into computer code. The main attributes of the notes are their type: full notes lasting a couple of seconds to sixteenth notes lasting about an eighth of a second. Equally important is their location on the scale which determines their pitch. Oftentimes, these notes are combined with other notes to form chords.

The music coder can also code other features under his/her control, such as the rhythm of the music, how loud it is played and whether to use sustain to lengthen the sound of the notes. To ease into the coding, I chose the simple song "When the Saints Go Marching in" which only uses white keys but has numerous chords. A much more difficult piece "Fur Elise" by Beethoven will be coded next in Chapter 13 after we have gained some experience with "Saints". I picked "Elise" because it has about all the unusual symbols that we are likely to encounter anywhere. In addition, the collection of songs provided with the Yamaha keyboard includes "Fur Elise". It is played by an excellent pianist who provides a good reference point for the beat, the volume and the pauses, which makes listening to it so enjoyable.

Fig 12.1 Sheet Music of "When the Saints Go Marching In"

The "Saints" Sheet Music

Above is one of the hundreds of arrangements of this popular traditional song. It is in C major (no black keys to play) it was composed in 1896 and it is in the public domain. I picked it out of my collection because it is used for beginners' piano lessons. It is easy to play and is loaded with chords which are one of our important coding challenges.

Coding the Song "Saints"

The general setup of this first page of sheet music shows four grand staffs (the usual way that piano music is presented). The fraction, 4/4, means that the quarter note has the beat and that there are 4 beats in each measure. Each measure will last 2 seconds if we set the beat at 120 beats per minute. Coding the 108 notes in the 16 measures requires 130 lines of code because chords require more lines of code than there are notes (some long notes in one staff have to be split into shorter notes to match the notes in the other staff).

When only one person is doing the coding, it can require a lot of looking from the sheet music to the charts to the PC screen making it easy to lose one's place and train of thought. I find it easier to make it a 2-step process. The first step involves determining the port number of each note. I make a copy of the sheet music and jot down the port numbers for both the white and black notes using the charts that we referred to. Once the port number of a note is coded in, the rest of the data can be pasted in and corrected as need be.

Let us code the first page of Saints one measure at a time and explain how to do the coding. In measure 1 we have a quarter rest then three quarter notes in the treble clef and three rests in the bass clef. Since the quarter rest and the three quarter notes will last two seconds at the 120 beat, there is no need to code anything from the bass clef. The first 4 lines of code will look like this:

//Measure 1

```
{0,0,0,0,0,0, BEAT_120, 0, 0, DURATION_QUARTER, SOLTIME_B, 0, BLACK_KEY },
{36,0,0,0,0,0, BEAT_120, 0, 0, DURATION_QUARTER, SOLTIME_B, 0, WHITE_KEY },
{38,0,0,0,0,0, BEAT_120, 0, 0, DURATION_QUARTER, SOLTIME_B, 0, WHITE_KEY },
{39,0,0,0,0,0, BEAT_120, 0, 0, DURATION_QUARTER, SOLTIME_B, 0, WHITE_KEY },
```

To recap the meaning of the information coded above, the first requirement is to select one of the Mega's ports to activate the appropriate solenoid. This port number is shown before the first comma. On the first line the number is zero which means that we want to pause for the duration of the selected note. In this case, it is a quarter note. To obtain the pause, we type in six 0's separated by commas. Port 0 is not used in the white keys and neither is binary 0 in the black keys. With no solenoid selected, a rest or pause will take place for 500ms. Next we have the beat which is 120 BPM (500 milliseconds per quarter note). Then two zeroes were chosen by the music coder to signify that the sustain feature is off and that the volume is normal. The soltime of the quarter note is set at a normal 75% (B). The next zero tells us that this note is not part of the chord. The final bit of information tells us whether the key is black or white.

If this seems like a lot of work for a pause, it is. But, as I mentioned before, we will find a lot of repetition and once familiar with the coding and the use of the editing functions in the Arduino software (they are the same as those found in "Word") it is a lot easier than it might seem. Except for the port numbers the next three lines are identical to the first line and can be copied and pasted in place. The port numbers are then corrected from the copy of the sheet music in the two-step coding method or directly from the sheet music when the direct method is used.

The printed lines in this book limit me to about 60 characters compared to the very long lines that can be written in the Arduino sketches. For the sake of clarity and brevity, I will abbreviate the coding of the chords as follows, (Remember, the abbreviations are not to be used when coding the songs in the Arduino sketches).

CHORD_START is abbreviated as: C_S

CHORD_CONTINUE is abbreviated as: C_C

CHORD_END is abbreviated as: C_E

As we saw in the first measure, when the note is not part of a chord, a zero is coded instead of the abbreviations described above.

//Measure 2

```
{40,0,0,0,0,0, BEAT_120, 0, 0, DURATION_QUARTER, SOLTIME_B, 0, WHITE_KEY },
{33,0,0,0,0,0, BEAT_120, 0, 0, DURATION_QUARTER, SOLTIME_B, C_S, WHITE_KEY },
{31,0,0,0,0,0, BEAT_120, 0, 0, DURATION_QUARTER, SOLTIME_B, C_C, WHITE_KEY },
{29,0,0,0,0,0, BEAT_120, 0, 0, DURATION_QUARTER, SOLTIME_B, C_E, WHITE_KEY },
{33,0,0,0,0,0, BEAT_120, 0, 0, DURATION_QUARTER, SOLTIME_B, C_S, WHITE_KEY },
{31,0,0,0,0,0, BEAT_120, 0, 0, DURATION_QUARTER, SOLTIME_B, C_C, WHITE_KEY },
{29,0,0,0,0,0, BEAT_120, 0, 0, DURATION_QUARTER, SOLTIME_B, C_E, WHITE_KEY },
{33,0,0,0,0,0, BEAT_120, 0, 0, DURATION_QUARTER, SOLTIME_B, C_S, WHITE_KEY },
{31,0,0,0,0,0, BEAT_120, 0, 0, DURATION_QUARTER, SOLTIME_B, C_C, WHITE_KEY },
{29,0,0,0,0,0, BEAT_120, 0, 0, DURATION_QUARTER, SOLTIME_B, C_E, WHITE_KEY },
```

Measure 2 has 10 notes. I cut and pasted the four notes from measure 1 and made the following changes to each line. In line 1, the black key port 0 was changed to white key port 40. In the next three lines, the white key port numbers were changed to 33, 31, and 29. The 0's indicating that the notes were not part of a cord were changed to C_S, C_C and C_E to indicate that the three notes make up a chord. The three lines were then copied and pasted two more times to complete the 10 line measure without further changes. Moving right along to measure 3, we paste one more set of three lines from measure 2 for the first chord. Then we go back to measure one and copy the second, third and fourth lines and paste them in after the chord which completes the coding of the six notes of measure 3.

//Measure 3

```
{33,0,0,0,0,0, BEAT_120, 0, 0, DURATION_QUARTER, SOLTIME_B, C_S, WHITE_KEY },
{31,0,0,0,0,0, BEAT_120, 0, 0, DURATION_QUARTER, SOLTIME_B, C_C, WHITE_KEY },
{29,0,0,0,0,0, BEAT_120, 0, 0, DURATION_QUARTER, SOLTIME_B, C_E, WHITE_KEY },
{36,0,0,0,0,0, BEAT_120, 0, 0, DURATION_QUARTER, SOLTIME_B, 0, WHITE_KEY },
{38,0,0,0,0,0, BEAT_120, 0, 0, DURATION_QUARTER, SOLTIME_B, 0, WHITE_KEY },
{39,0,0,0,0,0, BEAT_120, 0, 0, DURATION_QUARTER, SOLTIME_B, 0, WHITE_KEY },
```

Measure 4 is an exact duplicate of measure 2 and measure 5 is an exact duplicate of measure 3, so it is just a matter of copying and pasting these two measures into our music code.

//Measure 4

```
{40,0,0,0,0,0, BEAT_120, 0, 0, DURATION_QUARTER, SOLTIME_B, 0, WHITE_KEY },
{33,0,0,0,0,0, BEAT_120, 0, 0, DURATION_QUARTER, SOLTIME_B, C_S, WHITE_KEY },
{31,0,0,0,0,0, BEAT_120, 0, 0, DURATION_QUARTER, SOLTIME_B, C_C, WHITE_KEY },
{29,0,0,0,0,0, BEAT_120, 0, 0, DURATION_QUARTER, SOLTIME_B, C_E, WHITE_KEY },
{33,0,0,0,0,0, BEAT_120, 0, 0, DURATION_QUARTER, SOLTIME_B, C_S, WHITE_KEY },
{31,0,0,0,0,0, BEAT_120, 0, 0, DURATION_QUARTER, SOLTIME_B, C_C, WHITE_KEY },
{29,0,0,0,0,0, BEAT_120, 0, 0, DURATION_QUARTER, SOLTIME_B, C_E, WHITE_KEY },
{33,0,0,0,0,0, BEAT_120, 0, 0, DURATION_QUARTER, SOLTIME_B, C_S, WHITE_KEY },
{31,0,0,0,0,0, BEAT_120, 0, 0, DURATION_QUARTER, SOLTIME_B, C_C, WHITE_KEY },
{29,0,0,0,0,0, BEAT_120, 0, 0, DURATION_QUARTER, SOLTIME_B, C_E, WHITE_KEY },
```

//Measure 5

```
{33,0,0,0,0,0, BEAT_120, 0, 0, DURATION_QUARTER, SOLTIME_B, C_S, WHITE_KEY },
{31,0,0,0,0,0, BEAT_120, 0, 0, DURATION_QUARTER, SOLTIME_B, C_C, WHITE_KEY },
{29,0,0,0,0,0, BEAT_120, 0, 0, DURATION_QUARTER, SOLTIME_B, C_E, WHITE_KEY },
{36,0,0,0,0,0, BEAT_120, 0, 0, DURATION_QUARTER, SOLTIME_B, 0, WHITE_KEY },
```

```
{38,0,0,0,0,0, BEAT_120, 0, 0, DURATION_QUARTER, SOLTIME_B, 0, WHITE_KEY },
{39,0,0,0,0,0, BEAT_120, 0, 0, DURATION_QUARTER, SOLTIME_B, 0, WHITE_KEY },
```

Measures 6 and 7 are very similar having chords that are the same as the chords of measures 2 and 3, which means that we should be able to copy a number of lines of code. The half notes in the melody staff (played with the right hand) have the same time duration as two quarter notes played consecutively. To code these half notes, we will code a quarter note with a soltime of 100% (A) and a second quarter note with the normal soltime B. Because the Mega is so fast, the mini-robot will stay energized with the first quarter note and, before it finds out that anything is happening, the second quarter note will re-energize it as part of a chord. Coding the half note this way is exactly what we need so that we can play a four-note chord during the second quarter of the half notes. We will use the same technique to play the second half notes in measure 6 and the two half notes of measure 7.

To implement the coding of measures 6 and 7, we copy and paste the second line of measure 1 on the first and second lines of measure 6. On the first line, we need only to change the port number from 36 to 40 and the SOLTIME from B to A. On the second, we change the port number from 36 to 40 and also change the 0 in the chord location to C_S (CHORD_START) to indicate that this note is the first of a chord of four notes. In the third line, (of the first three chord lines pasted from measure 2), the C_S is changed to C_C (CHORD_CONTINUE). The fourth and fifth lines are correct as they were pasted.

The easiest way to complete the other five lines in measure 6 is to cut and paste the first five lines and change the port number 40 to port number 38. Everything else is correct as pasted.

//Measure 6

```
{40,0,0,0,0,0, BEAT_120, 0, 0, DURATION_QUARTER, SOLTIME_A, 0, WHITE_KEY },
{40,0,0,0,0,0, BEAT_120, 0, 0, DURATION_QUARTER, SOLTIME_B, C_S, WHITE_KEY },
```

{33,0,0,0,0,0, BEAT_120, 0, 0, DURATION_QUARTER, SOLTIME_B, C_C, WHITE_KEY },
{31,0,0,0,0,0, BEAT_120, 0, 0, DURATION_QUARTER, SOLTIME_B, C_C, WHITE_KEY },
{29,0,0,0,0,0, BEAT_120, 0, 0, DURATION_QUARTER, SOLTIME_B, C_E, WHITE_KEY },
{38,0,0,0,0,0, BEAT_120, 0, 0, DURATION_QUARTER, SOLTIME_A, 0, WHITE_KEY },
{38,0,0,0,0,0, BEAT_120, 0, 0, DURATION_QUARTER, SOLTIME_B, C_S, WHITE_KEY },
{33,0,0,0,0,0, BEAT_120, 0, 0, DURATION_QUARTER, SOLTIME_B, C_C, WHITE_KEY },
{31,0,0,0,0,0, BEAT_120, 0, 0, DURATION_QUARTER, SOLTIME_B, C_C, WHITE_KEY },
{29,0,0,0,0,0, BEAT_120, 0, 0, DURATION_QUARTER, SOLTIME_B, C_E, WHITE_KEY },

Measure 7 is a snap. Copy and paste measure 6 and change the ports on lines one and two from 38 to 36. Everything else is exactly the same.

//Measure 7

{36,0,0,0,0,0, BEAT_120, 0, 0, DURATION_QUARTER, SOLTIME_A, 0, WHITE_KEY },
{36,0,0,0,0,0, BEAT_120, 0, 0, DURATION_QUARTER, SOLTIME_B, C_S, WHITE_KEY },
{33,0,0,0,0,0, BEAT_120, 0, 0, DURATION_QUARTER, SOLTIME_B, C_C, WHITE_KEY },
{31,0,0,0,0,0, BEAT_120, 0, 0, DURATION_QUARTER, SOLTIME_B, C_C, WHITE_KEY },
{29,0,0,0,0,0, BEAT_120, 0, 0, DURATION_QUARTER, SOLTIME_B, C_E, WHITE_KEY },
{38,0,0,0,0,0, BEAT_120, 0, 0, DURATION_QUARTER, SOLTIME_A, 0, WHITE_KEY },
{38,0,0,0,0,0, BEAT_120, 0, 0, DURATION_QUARTER, SOLTIME_B, C_S, WHITE_KEY },
{33,0,0,0,0,0, BEAT_120, 0, 0, DURATION_QUARTER, SOLTIME_B, C_C, WHITE_KEY },
{31,0,0,0,0,0, BEAT_120, 0, 0, DURATION_QUARTER, SOLTIME_B, C_C, WHITE_KEY },
{29,0,0,0,0,0, BEAT_120, 0, 0, DURATION_QUARTER, SOLTIME_B, C_E, WHITE_KEY },

Measure 8 is unique in that it has a full note covering the entire two-second duration of the measure. The full note will be split into four quarter notes. The first three of these quarter notes will have a soltime of 100% (A) so that all four will play without interruption because the solenoid will stay energized. The last one will have a normal 75% soltime (B).

One way to implement the coding of this long measure of 13 lines is to copy and paste the first four lines of measure 2 or 4. The port number must be changed to 37 and the soltime to A. This line is then copied and pasted as line 2. The only additional change needed to line 2 is to replace the 0 in the chord position with C_S. The port numbers of the three other chord lines of code are 33, 32 and 28. One more change in these first five lines must be done, the C_S of the third line needs to be changed to C_C. Lines 2, 3, 4 and 5 are then copied as a group and pasted in the next four lines twice. Only one change is needed in these eight lines, the soltime in line 10 is changed to a B instead of an A.

```
//Measure 8

{37,0,0,0,0,0, BEAT_120, 0, 0, DURATION_QUARTER, SOLTIME_A, 0, WHITE_KEY },
{37,0,0,0,0,0, BEAT_120, 0, 0, DURATION_QUARTER, SOLTIME_A, C_S, WHITE_KEY },
{33,0,0,0,0,0, BEAT_120, 0, 0, DURATION_QUARTER, SOLTIME_A, C_C, WHITE_KEY },
{32,0,0,0,0,0, BEAT_120, 0, 0, DURATION_QUARTER, SOLTIME_A, C_C, WHITE_KEY },
{28,0,0,0,0,0, BEAT_120, 0, 0, DURATION_QUARTER, SOLTIME_A, C_E, WHITE_KEY },
{37,0,0,0,0,0, BEAT_120, 0, 0, DURATION_QUARTER, SOLTIME_A, C_S, WHITE_KEY },
{33,0,0,0,0,0, BEAT_120, 0, 0, DURATION_QUARTER, SOLTIME_A, C_C, WHITE_KEY },
{32,0,0,0,0,0, BEAT_120, 0, 0, DURATION_QUARTER, SOLTIME_A, C_C, WHITE_KEY },
{28,0,0,0,0,0, BEAT_120, 0, 0, DURATION_QUARTER, SOLTIME_A, C_E, WHITE_KEY },
{37,0,0,0,0,0, BEAT_120, 0, 0, DURATION_QUARTER, SOLTIME_B, C_S, WHITE_KEY },
{33,0,0,0,0,0, BEAT_120, 0, 0, DURATION_QUARTER, SOLTIME_B, C_C, WHITE_KEY },
{32,0,0,0,0,0, BEAT_120, 0, 0, DURATION_QUARTER, SOLTIME_B, C_C, WHITE_KEY },
{28,0,0,0,0,0, BEAT_120, 0, 0, DURATION_QUARTER, SOLTIME_B, C_E, WHITE_KEY },
```

One half of the page of music has been completed with 69 lines of code. Only one different new cord will have to be coded in the next eight measures which means that we'll be able to do a good deal more copying and pasting.

Measure 9 uses the same chord as found in measure 8; it provides the beat as the first notes of the measure. We copy and paste it in, then we paste in 3 quarter notes from measure 1 and change the port numbers to 38, 38, and 37.

//Measure 9

```
{33,0,0,0,0,0, BEAT_120, 0, 0, DURATION_QUARTER, SOLTIME_B, C_S, WHITE_KEY },
{32,0,0,0,0,0, BEAT_120, 0, 0, DURATION_QUARTER, SOLTIME_B, C_C, WHITE_KEY },
{28,0,0,0,0,0, BEAT_120, 0, 0, DURATION_QUARTER, SOLTIME_B, C_E, WHITE_KEY },
{38,0,0,0,0,0, BEAT_120, 0, 0, DURATION_QUARTER, SOLTIME_B, 0, WHITE_KEY },
{38,0,0,0,0,0, BEAT_120, 0, 0, DURATION_QUARTER, SOLTIME_B, 0, WHITE_KEY },
{37,0,0,0,0,0, BEAT_120, 0, 0, DURATION_QUARTER, SOLTIME_B, 0, WHITE_KEY },
```

Measures 10 and 11 are a little tricky because the chords at the beginning of the measures are full notes with a duration that lasts the entire measure. After the initial half of the chord is played, the half note in the melody staff is played out. At this point we will have to code quarter notes for the rest of the measure. The full note chord will have to be divided into a half note chord and two quarter note chords to match the notes in the melody staff. To make sure that the solenoids are energized for the duration of a full note, 100% soltime (SOLTIME_A) will be coded in the notes making up the chord for the first half of the chord plus one quarter note. The last quarter note will have a SOLTIME B for both measures.

We will copy lines 2, 3, 4, and 5 of measure 6 but we have to make a few changes. On the first line, port 40 becomes port 36. The other 3 ports are correct. The duration of these four lines is changed from quarter to half and the soltime is changed from B to A. Now, copy and paste these four lines twice more and make the following changes to the next eight lines:

Turn line 5 into a pause by changing the port number to 0 and changing white key to black key. By chance, line 9 has the correct port number. The duration of all eight notes needs to be changed back to quarter note from half note. The soltime of the bottom 4 lines (9, 10, 11 and 12) must be changed from A to B.

//Measure 10

```
{36,0,0,0,0,0, BEAT_120, 0, 0, DURATION_HALF, SOLTIME_A, C_S, WHITE_KEY },
{33,0,0,0,0,0, BEAT_120, 0, 0, DURATION_HALF, SOLTIME_A, C_C, WHITE_KEY },
{31,0,0,0,0,0, BEAT_120, 0, 0, DURATION_HALF, SOLTIME_A, C_C, WHITE_KEY },
{29,0,0,0,0,0, BEAT_120, 0, 0, DURATION_HALF, SOLTIME_A, C_E, WHITE_KEY },
{0,0,0,0,0,0, BEAT_120, 0, 0, DURATION_QUARTER, SOLTIME_A, C_S, BLACK_KEY },
{33,0,0,0,0,0, BEAT_120, 0, 0, DURATION_QUARTER, SOLTIME_A, C_C, WHITE_KEY },
{31,0,0,0,0,0, BEAT_120, 0, 0, DURATION_QUARTER, SOLTIME_A, C_C, WHITE_KEY },
{29,0,0,0,0,0, BEAT_120, 0, 0, DURATION_QUARTER, SOLTIME_A, C_E, WHITE_KEY },
{36,0,0,0,0,0, BEAT_120, 0, 0, DURATION_QUARTER, SOLTIME_B, C_S, WHITE_KEY },
{33,0,0,0,0,0, BEAT_120, 0, 0, DURATION_QUARTER, SOLTIME_B, C_C, WHITE_KEY },
{31,0,0,0,0,0, BEAT_120, 0, 0, DURATION_QUARTER, SOLTIME_B, C_C, WHITE_KEY },
{29,0,0,0,0,0, BEAT_120, 0, 0, DURATION_QUARTER, SOLTIME_B, C_E, WHITE_KEY },.
```

Measure 11 is very similar to measure 10, so let's copy and paste all 12 lines of code from measure 10 and make the following easy changes.

The half note on the first line gets a different port number: 38.

The port number of line 5 and of line 9 becomes port number 40 and the color of line 5 goes back to white.

//Measure 11

```
{38,0,0,0,0,0, BEAT_120, 0, 0, DURATION_HALF, SOLTIME_A, C_S, WHITE_KEY },
{33,0,0,0,0,0, BEAT_120, 0, 0, DURATION_HALF, SOLTIME_A, C_C, WHITE_KEY },
{31,0,0,0,0,0, BEAT_120, 0, 0, DURATION_HALF, SOLTIME_A, C_C, WHITE_KEY },
{29,0,0,0,0,0, BEAT_120, 0, 0, DURATION_HALF, SOLTIME_A, C_E, WHITE_KEY },
{40,0,0,0,0,0, BEAT_120, 0, 0, DURATION_QUARTER, SOLTIME_A, C_S, WHITE_KEY },
{33,0,0,0,0,0, BEAT_120, 0, 0, DURATION_QUARTER, SOLTIME_A, C_C, WHITE_KEY },
{31,0,0,0,0,0, BEAT_120, 0, 0, DURATION_QUARTER, SOLTIME_A, C_C, WHITE_KEY },
{29,0,0,0,0,0, BEAT_120, 0, 0, DURATION_QUARTER, SOLTIME_A, C_E, WHITE_KEY },
{40,0,0,0,0,0, BEAT_120, 0, 0, DURATION_QUARTER, SOLTIME_B, C_S, WHITE_KEY },
{33,0,0,0,0,0, BEAT_120, 0, 0, DURATION_QUARTER, SOLTIME_B, C_C, WHITE_KEY },
{31,0,0,0,0,0, BEAT_120, 0, 0, DURATION_QUARTER, SOLTIME_B, C_C, WHITE_KEY },
{29,0,0,0,0,0, BEAT_120, 0, 0, DURATION_QUARTER, SOLTIME_B, C_E, WHITE_KEY },
```

Measure 12 is also close enough to measure 10 to copy and paste it and make a number of changes.

Fist line: change port 36 to 40.

First four lines: change the duration to quarter.

Second and third lines: change ports 33 and 31 to ports 34 and 32.

Fifth line; change the port number to 39 and the color of the key to white.

Sixth and seventh lines: change ports 33 and 31 to ports 34 and 32.

Fifth to eighth lines: change duration from quarter to half.

Delete line 9

Tenth and eleventh line: change ports 33 and 31 to ports 34 and 32

//Measure 12

```
{40,0,0,0,0,0, BEAT_120, 0, 0, DURATION_QUARTER, SOLTIME_A, C_S, WHITE_KEY },
{34,0,0,0,0,0, BEAT_120, 0, 0, DURATION_QUARTER, SOLTIME_A, C_C, WHITE_KEY },
{32,0,0,0,0,0, BEAT_120, 0, 0, DURATION_QUARTER, SOLTIME_A, C_C, WHITE_KEY },
{29,0,0,0,0,0, BEAT_120, 0, 0, DURATION_QUARTER, SOLTIME_A, C_E, WHITE_KEY },
{39,0,0,0,0,0, BEAT_120, 0, 0, DURATION_HALF, SOLTIME_A, C_S, WHITE_KEY },
{34,0,0,0,0,0, BEAT_120, 0, 0, DURATION_HALF, SOLTIME_A, C_C, WHITE_KEY },
{32,0,0,0,0,0, BEAT_120, 0, 0, DURATION_HALF, SOLTIME_A, C_C, WHITE_KEY },
{29,0,0,0,0,0, BEAT_120, 0, 0, DURATION_HALF, SOLTIME_A, C_E, WHITE_KEY },
{34,0,0,0,0,0, BEAT_120, 0, 0, DURATION_QUARTER, SOLTIME_B, C_S, WHITE_KEY },
{32,0,0,0,0,0, BEAT_120, 0, 0, DURATION_QUARTER, SOLTIME_B, C_C, WHITE_KEY },
{29,0,0,0,0,0, BEAT_120, 0, 0, DURATION_QUARTER, SOLTIME_B, C_E, WHITE_KEY },
```

The half notes of measure 13 are similar to the sixth, seventh and eighth notes of measure 12 so let's copy and paste them in lines 1 through 3. The last two quarter notes are the same as the last two notes of measure 5, so let's paste them in. The soltime for all notes in measure 13 are B's so we'll make those changes as well.

//Measure 13

```
{34,0,0,0,0,0, BEAT_120, 0, 0, DURATION_HALF, SOLTIME_B, C_S, WHITE_KEY },
{32,0,0,0,0,0, BEAT_120, 0, 0, DURATION_HALF, SOLTIME_B, C_C, WHITE_KEY },
{29,0,0,0,0,0, BEAT_120, 0, 0, DURATION_HALF, SOLTIME_B, C_E, WHITE_KEY },
{38,0,0,0,0,0, BEAT_120, 0, 0, DURATION_QUARTER, SOLTIME_B, 0, WHITE_KEY },
{39,0,0,0,0,0, BEAT_120, 0, 0, DURATION_QUARTER, SOLTIME_B, 0, WHITE_KEY },
```

The notes in the chords of measure 14 are the same as the chords of measure 10, so we will copy the first four lines and paste them in measure 14. The port of the first line becomes port number 40. All soltimes in the measure need to be changed to B's. The four lines can then be copied and pasted in the next four lines with just one change: the port number of line 5 is changed from 40 to 38.

//Measure 14

```
{40,0,0,0,0,0, BEAT_120, 0, 0, DURATION_HALF, SOLTIME_B, C_S, WHITE_KEY },
{33,0,0,0,0,0, BEAT_120, 0, 0, DURATION_HALF, SOLTIME_B, C_C, WHITE_KEY },
{31,0,0,0,0,0, BEAT_120, 0, 0, DURATION_HALF, SOLTIME_B, C_C, WHITE_KEY },
{29,0,0,0,0,0, BEAT_120, 0, 0, DURATION_HALF, SOLTIME_B, C_E, WHITE_KEY },
{38,0,0,0,0,0, BEAT_120, 0, 0, DURATION_HALF, SOLTIME_B, C_S, WHITE_KEY },
{33,0,0,0,0,0, BEAT_120, 0, 0, DURATION_HALF, SOLTIME_B, C_C, WHITE_KEY },
{31,0,0,0,0,0, BEAT_120, 0, 0, DURATION_HALF, SOLTIME_B, C_C, WHITE_KEY },
{29,0,0,0,0,0, BEAT_120, 0, 0, DURATION_HALF, SOLTIME_B, C_E, WHITE_KEY },
```

The first half of measure 15 has the same chord as measure 13, so those 3 lines can be copied and pasted in lines 2, 3 and 4. For line 1 copy and paste line 2 and make two changes: port 34 becomes port 36 and C_S in line 2 becomes a C_C. The second half has a chord used in measure 9. First, copy and paste the first line of this measure and change the port from 36 to 37. Then copy the first three lines of measure 9 and paste them with the following changes: line 6 needs

163

a C_C instead of a C_S and the duration has to be changed from quarter to half. All soltimes in this measure are B's.

//Measure 15

```
{36,0,0,0,0,0, BEAT_120, 1, 0, DURATION_HALF, SOLTIME_B, C_S, WHITE_KEY },
{34,0,0,0,0,0, BEAT_120, 1, 0, DURATION_HALF, SOLTIME_B, C_C, WHITE_KEY },
{32,0,0,0,0,0, BEAT_120, 1, 0, DURATION_HALF, SOLTIME_B, C_C, WHITE_KEY },
{29,0,0,0,0,0, BEAT_120, 1, 0, DURATION_HALF, SOLTIME_B, C_E, WHITE_KEY },
{37,0,0,0,0,0, BEAT_120, 1, 0, DURATION_HALF, SOLTIME_B, C_S, WHITE_KEY },
{33,0,0,0,0,0, BEAT_120, 1, 0, DURATION_HALF, SOLTIME_B, C_C, WHITE_KEY },
{32,0,0,0,0,0, BEAT_120, 1, 0, DURATION_HALF, SOLTIME_B, C_C, WHITE_KEY },
{28,0,0,0,0,0, BEAT_120, 1, 0, DURATION_HALF, SOLTIME_B, C_E, WHITE_KEY },
```

Measure 16 is easy: copy and paste the first four lines of measure 14, change the durations from half to full and change the port number on the first line from 40 to 36. I activated the sustain function in the last two measures and added a line of code after measure 16 to indicate the end of the song and to turn off sustain. The new line of code has 11 zeroes between SONG_END and WHITE_KEY separated with commas.

```
{36,0,0,0,0,0, BEAT_120, 1, 0, DURATION_FULL, SOLTIME_A, C_S, WHITE_KEY },
{33,0,0,0,0,0, BEAT_120, 1, 0, DURATION_FULL, SOLTIME_A, C_C, WHITE_KEY },
{31,0,0,0,0,0, BEAT_120, 1, 0, DURATION_FULL, SOLTIME_A, C_C, WHITE_KEY },
{29,0,0,0,0,0, BEAT_120, 1, 0, DURATION_FULL, SOLTIME_A, C_E, WHITE_KEY },

{SONG_END,0,0,0,0,0,0,0,0,0,0,0,WHITE_KEY}
```

Coding a Song

Coding this song without looking at the instructions would be an excellent exercise. It does take a lot of concentration to keep the mistakes to a minimum. The compiler will pick up most of them but it cannot know, for instance, if you put in the wrong port number (a very common mistake of mine because of all the copying and pasting) so you must be careful about that. Two people doing the coding together will speed things up and reduce the error count.

I use a simple device to help me keep track of the measure that I am working on. By cutting out a rectangle about 2 inches long (or the average size of a measure) and an inch deep out of the top of a sheet of paper, it is possible to show the measure that I am working on while covering the measures on each side. It makes it much easier to find my place again after I look away.

When working alone, I code the song in two steps. First, I add the port number of each note on a copy of the sheet music. Then, I use this information to type in the ports in the sketch. The rest of that particular line of code can be pasted in and corrected if need be. I find this two-step method easier than typing in the entire line of code directly from the sheet music. Nevertheless, it is a time consuming exercise; with a few hours of practice, two people should be able to code a sheet of music in two hours, while one person might take three hours.

Summary of Chapter 12

Chapter 12 described the coding of the simple song, "When the Saints Go Marching in" which is often used to teach beginners how to play the piano. Here we used it to teach ourselves how to translate sheet music symbols into computer code. "Saints" has enough different chords that many configurations can be practiced. There are no accidentals to contend with, so we will leave that interesting challenge for the next chapter.

16 measures and 130 notes were coded. For this page of music, 936 bytes out of 256,000 were used to store "Saints" in the Mega's memory. The storage of the Robo sketch code requires approximately 2000 more bytes but this same sketch code is used for all the songs that are uploaded at one time. Playing "Saints" at 140 BPM, the duration of the first page is about 25 seconds.

These 16 measures of music code may be used to build a new Arduino sketch called "MPP Saints from Book 2.0" according to the instructions in Chapter 15. The abbreviations must be expanded and the music code would replace the music code found in a sketch such as MPP Elise Diagnostic 10.0. This sketch "MPP Saints from Book 2.0" can also be downloaded from my website modernplayerpiano.com.

At that rate (936 bytes lasting 25 seconds), the Mega's memory can accommodate 114 minutes of music.

Beethoven's "Fur Elise" will be coded in the next Chapter.

CHAPTER 13

Coding "Fur Elise"

Now that we understand the basics of coding music, we will code the first page of Beethoven's "Fur Elise." This piece is much more difficult to play than Saints but not much more difficult to code although there are some new features to learn. Most of the notes are eighth notes, so the pianist has to play fast to keep up with the beat (not a problem for our mini-robots!). A friend of mine told me that when he learned to play the piano he had to practice this very piece every day for a year before he felt confident that he was playing it correctly. Coding it is a piece of cake compared to that ordeal!

Coding the Song "Elise"

The 3/4 fraction here tells us that the quarter note has the beat and that "Elise" is played in three quarter time (like a waltz). Not much help from the words "Poco Moto" to tell us what the beat is so, we will try 110 BPM as a starting point. The letters *pp* tells us that the volume is somewhat less than average. When typing "Poco Moto" into Google, you get all sorts of answers about the tempo of "Elise"—some of them are very funny, but no signs of a metronome number that we can use. There is also a wealth of information about who the mysterious Elise might have been. And, of course there are numerous versions of the song "Fur Elise," including a 60-minute rendition with a full orchestra in the background.

Fig 13.1 Sheet Music of "Fur Elise"
Courtesy of www.mistrelpress.com

We will code the first page (see Fig 13.1 above) of "Elise" as we did with "Saints." I coded this fairly difficult piece using the two-step method where the port numbers are noted on a copy of the page of sheet music. This page has 20 measures and 130 notes to be coded, but because of the numerous chords it requires 200 lines of code. This is a few more than "Saints," but because the first

8 measures are played twice it requires more than 40 seconds to play (most songs run two to three minutes in their entirety). Most of the measures of "Elise" have six eighth notes to make up the equivalent of three quarter notes as dictated by the 3/4 fraction. In Chapter 15 we will use these coded measures to build a music sketch which will be called "MPP Elise from Book".

The first measure only has two notes but we immediately bump into an accidental. It is the sharp next to white key D (#28, port # 44)— black key # 20. From the charts in Fig 11.1, Fig 7.1, or Photo 11.1, we determine that its port number in octal is 24, which is equal to "10 100" in binary. Make a note of this port number on the copy of the sheet music—we will see this note many more times. As with "Saints," we will abbreviate the words referring to the chords. The two lines of code for measure 1 look like this.

//Measure 1

```
{45,0,0,0,0,0, BEAT_110, 0, 0, DURATION_EIGHTH, SOLTIME_B, 0, WHITE_KEY },
{0,1,0,1,0,0, BEAT_110, 0, 0, DURATION_EIGHTH, SOLTIME_B, 0, BLACK_KEY },
```

In measure 2, the right hand does all the work playing the melody since we have nothing but a long pause in the bass staff. The melody consists of six eighth notes one of which is an accidental. This very same measure is repeated two more times on this page.

The designation for a sharp closely resembles a number sign (#), and it is active for the entire measure once it is displayed. In this case, it applies to the second note (another D) in the measure. But notice that there is a second D in this measure and that this second D is a natural. In order to cancel the effect of the first #, a new symbol resembling a b with a tail at the bottom disables the previous #. The third symbol having to do with accidentals also looks like a b (without the tail), and it tells us that the next note is a flat. Remember that a sharp or flat (a black note) is higher or lower by ½ pitch compared to the natural (white note) next to it. There are no flats in the music on this page, but they would be coded the same way as the sharps. The line of code for this sharp is the same as for the sharp in measure 1, so it can be copied and pasted.

//Measure 2

```
{45,0,0,0,0,0, BEAT_110, 0, 0, DURATION_EIGHTH, SOLTIME_B, 0, WHITE_KEY },
{0,1,0,1,0,0, BEAT_110, 0, 0, DURATION_EIGHTH, SOLTIME_B, 0, BLACK_KEY },
{45,0,0,0,0,0, BEAT_110, 0, 0, DURATION_EIGHTH, SOLTIME_B, 0, WHITE_KEY },
{42,0,0,0,0,0, BEAT_110, 0, 0, DURATION_EIGHTH, SOLTIME_B, 0, WHITE_KEY },
{44,0,0,0,0,0, BEAT_110, 0, 0, DURATION_EIGHTH, SOLTIME_B, 0, WHITE_KEY },
{43,0,0,0,0,0, BEAT_110, 0, 0, DURATION_EIGHTH, SOLTIME_B, 0, WHITE_KEY },
```

Measure 3 is the first of a dozen measures with a two-note chord as the first note. It is used to emphasize the beat. In most cases, they are quarter notes combined with eighth notes. The quarter note will be divided into two eighth notes of which the first one will have a soltime of 100% (A) so that it will play continuously until the second eighth note comes along to re-energize the solenoid.

//Measure 3

```
{41,0,0,0,0,0, BEAT_110, 0, 0, DURATION_EIGHTH, SOLTIME_A, C_S, WHITE_KEY },
{27,0,0,0,0,0, BEAT_110, 0, 0, DURATION_EIGHTH, SOLTIME_A, C_E, WHITE_KEY },
{41,0,0,0,0,0, BEAT_110, 0, 0, DURATION_EIGHTH, SOLTIME_B, C_S, WHITE_KEY },
{31,0,0,0,0,0, BEAT_110, 0, 0, DURATION_EIGHTH, SOLTIME_B, C_E, WHITE_KEY },
{34,0,0,0,0,0, BEAT_110, 0, 0, DURATION_EIGHTH, SOLTIME_B, 0, WHITE_KEY },
{36,0,0,0,0,0, BEAT_110, 0, 0, DURATION_EIGHTH, SOLTIME_B, 0, WHITE_KEY },
{38,0,0,0,0,0, BEAT_110, 0, 0, DURATION_EIGHTH, SOLTIME_B, 0, WHITE_KEY },
{41,0,0,0,0,0, BEAT_110, 0, 0, DURATION_EIGHTH, SOLTIME_B, 0, WHITE_KEY },
```

Except for the accidentals, measures 4 and 5 are very much like measure 3. The eight notes can be copied and pasted but the port numbers must be changed appropriately.

//Measure 4

```
{42,0,0,0,0,0, BEAT_110, 0, 0, DURATION_EIGHTH, SOLTIME_A, C_S, WHITE_KEY },
{24,0,0,0,0,0, BEAT_110, 0, 0, DURATION_EIGHTH, SOLTIME_A, C_E, WHITE_KEY },
{42,0,0,0,0,0, BEAT_110, 0, 0, DURATION_EIGHTH, SOLTIME_B, C_S WHITE_KEY },
{31,0,0,0,0,0, BEAT_110, 0, 0, DURATION_EIGHTH, SOLTIME_B, C_E, WHITE_KEY },
{0,0,1,1,0,0, BEAT_110, 0, 0, DURATION_EIGHTH, SOLTIME_B, 0, BLACK_KEY },
{38,0,0,0,0,0, BEAT_110, 0, 0, DURATION_EIGHTH, SOLTIME_B, 0, WHITE_KEY },
{0,1,0,0,0,1, BEAT_110, 0, 0, DURATION_EIGHTH, SOLTIME_B, 0, BLACK_KEY },
{42,0,0,0,0,0, BEAT_110, 0, 0, DURATION_EIGHTH, SOLTIME_B, 0, WHITE_KEY },
```

//Measure 5

```
{43,0,0,0,0,0, BEAT_110, 0, 0, DURATION_EIGHTH, SOLTIME_A, C_S, WHITE_KEY },
{27,0,0,0,0,0, BEAT_110, 0, 0, DURATION_EIGHTH, SOLTIME_A, C_E, WHITE_KEY },
{43,0,0,0,0,0, BEAT_110, 0, 0, DURATION_EIGHTH, SOLTIME_B, C_S, WHITE_KEY },
{31,0,0,0,0,0, BEAT_110, 0, 0, DURATION_EIGHTH, SOLTIME_B, C_E, WHITE_KEY },
{34,0,0,0,0,0, BEAT_110, 0, 0, DURATION_EIGHTH, SOLTIME_B, 0, WHITE_KEY },
{38,0,0,0,0,0, BEAT_110, 0, 0, DURATION_EIGHTH, SOLTIME_B, 0, WHITE_KEY },
{45,0,0,0,0,0, BEAT_110, 0, 0, DURATION_EIGHTH, SOLTIME_B, 0, WHITE_KEY },
{0,1,0,1,0,0, BEAT_110, 0, 0, DURATION_EIGHTH, SOLTIME_B, 0, BLACK_KEY },
```

Measure 6 is an exact duplicate of measure 2, and measure 7 is an exact duplicate of measure 3. You know what to do: copy and paste these 2 measures along with the measure numbers, which will be changed to 6 and 7.

//Measure 6

```
{45,0,0,0,0,0, BEAT_110, 0, 0, DURATION_EIGHTH, SOLTIME_B, 0, WHITE_KEY },
{0,1,0,1,0,0, BEAT_110, 0, 0, DURATION_EIGHTH, SOLTIME_B, 0, BLACK_KEY },
{45,0,0,0,0,0, BEAT_110, 0, 0, DURATION_EIGHTH, SOLTIME_B,0, WHITE_KEY },
{42,0,0,0,0,0, BEAT_110, 0, 0, DURATION_EIGHTH, SOLTIME_B, 0, WHITE_KEY },
{44,0,0,0,0,0, BEAT_110, 0, 0, DURATION_EIGHTH, SOLTIME_B, 0, WHITE_KEY },
{43,0,0,0,0,0, BEAT_110, 0, 0, DURATION_EIGHTH, SOLTIME_B, 0, WHITE_KEY },
```

//Measure 7

```
{41,0,0,0,0,0, BEAT_110, 0, 0, DURATION_EIGHTH, SOLTIME_A, C_S, WHITE_KEY },
{27,0,0,0,0,0, BEAT_110, 0, 0, DURATION_EIGHTH, SOLTIME_A, C_E, WHITE_KEY },
{41,0,0,0,0,0, BEAT_110, 0, 0, DURATION_EIGHTH, SOLTIME_B, C_S WHITE_KEY },
{31,0,0,0,0,0, BEAT_110, 0, 0, DURATION_EIGHTH, SOLTIME_B, C_E, WHITE_KEY },
{34,0,0,0,0,0, BEAT_110, 0, 0, DURATION_EIGHTH, SOLTIME_B, 0, WHITE_KEY },
{36,0,0,0,0,0, BEAT_110, 0, 0, DURATION_EIGHTH, SOLTIME_B, 0, WHITE_KEY },
{38,0,0,0,0,0, BEAT_110, 0, 0, DURATION_EIGHTH, SOLTIME_B, 0, WHITE_KEY },
{41,0,0,0,0,0, BEAT_110, 0, 0, DURATION_EIGHTH, SOLTIME_B, 0, WHITE_KEY },
```

Measure 8 is almost the same as measure 4 except for the fourth and fifth notes. Copy and paste measure 4 and make the two applicable changes.

//Measure 8

```
{42,0,0,0,0,0, BEAT_110, 0, 0, DURATION_EIGHTH, SOLTIME_A, C_S, WHITE_KEY },
{24,0,0,0,0,0, BEAT_110, 0, 0, DURATION_EIGHTH, SOLTIME_A, C_E, WHITE_KEY },
{42,0,0,0,0,0, BEAT_110, 0, 0, DURATION_EIGHTH, SOLTIME_B, C_S, WHITE_KEY },
{31,0,0,0,0,0, BEAT_110, 0, 0, DURATION_EIGHTH, SOLTIME_B, C_E, WHITE_KEY },
{0,0,1,1,0,0, BEAT_110, 0, 0, DURATION_EIGHTH, SOLTIME_B, 0, BLACK_KEY },
{37,0,0,0,0,0, BEAT_110, 0, 0, DURATION_EIGHTH, SOLTIME_B, 0, WHITE_KEY },
{43,0,0,0,0,0, BEAT_110, 0, 0, DURATION_EIGHTH, SOLTIME_B, 0, WHITE_KEY },
{42,0,0,0,0,0, BEAT_110, 0, 0, DURATION_EIGHTH, SOLTIME_B, 0, WHITE_KEY },
```

Something interesting happens when measure 9 is played. There is a double vertical line at the end which means that all eight previous measures are played a second time. But notice the 1 and 2 in the brackets above the staff. This means that on the first pass we play measure 9 and on the second pass we skip measure 9 and play measure 10 instead. Notice also that measure 9 is short two notes having only four eighth notes instead of six. But everything will come out right when we add the 2 notes from measure 1. To code measure 9, copy and paste the first two notes of measure 7 three times. The result is that half note 41 is split into four eighth notes, three of them are paired with other eighth notes to form three two-note chords. The last 41 is a single one eighth note constructed with a soltime B and a zero at the chord location. Next, the two notes from measure 1 are added at the end.

The first eight measures are repeated after measure 9. Measure 9 is then skipped the second time around and we code measure 10.

//Measure 9

```
{41,0,0,0,0,0, BEAT_110, 0, 0, DURATION_EIGHTH, SOLTIME_A, C_S, WHITE_KEY },
{27,0,0,0,0,0, BEAT_110, 0, 0, DURATION_EIGHTH, SOLTIME_A, C_E, WHITE_KEY },
{41,0,0,0,0,0, BEAT_110, 0, 0, DURATION_EIGHTH, SOLTIME_A, C_S, WHITE_KEY },
{31,0,0,0,0,0, BEAT_110, 0, 0, DURATION_EIGHTH, SOLTIME_A, C_E, WHITE_KEY },
{41,0,0,0,0,0, BEAT_110, 0, 0, DURATION_EIGHTH, SOLTIME_A, C_S, WHITE_KEY },
{34,0,0,0,0,0, BEAT_110, 0, 0, DURATION_EIGHTH, SOLTIME_A, C_E, WHITE_KEY },
{41,0,0,0,0,0, BEAT_110, 0, 0, DURATION_EIGHTH, SOLTIME_B, 0, WHITE_KEY },
{45,0,0,0,0,0, BEAT_110, 0, 0, DURATION_EIGHTH, SOLTIME_B, 0, WHITE_KEY },
{0,1,0,1,0,0, BEAT_110, 0, 0, DURATION_EIGHTH, SOLTIME_B, 0, BLACK_KEY },
```

//Measure 2 (Repeat)

```
{45,0,0,0,0,0, BEAT_110, 0, 0, DURATION_EIGHTH, SOLTIME_B, 0, WHITE_KEY },
{0,1,0,1,0,0, BEAT_110, 0, 0, DURATION_EIGHTH, SOLTIME_B, 0, BLACK_KEY },
{45,0,0,0,0,0, BEAT_110, 0, 0, DURATION_EIGHTH, SOLTIME_B,0, WHITE_KEY },
{42,0,0,0,0,0, BEAT_110, 0, 0, DURATION_EIGHTH, SOLTIME_B, 0, WHITE_KEY },
{44,0,0,0,0,0, BEAT_110, 0, 0, DURATION_EIGHTH, SOLTIME_B, 0, WHITE_KEY },
{43,0,0,0,0,0, BEAT_110, 0, 0, DURATION_EIGHTH, SOLTIME_B, 0, WHITE_KEY },
```

//Measure 3 (Repeat)

```
{41,0,0,0,0,0, BEAT_110, 0, 0, DURATION_EIGHTH, SOLTIME_A, C_S, WHITE_KEY },
{27,0,0,0,0,0, BEAT_110, 0, 0, DURATION_EIGHTH, SOLTIME_A, C_E, WHITE_KEY },
{41,0,0,0,0,0, BEAT_110, 0, 0, DURATION_EIGHTH, SOLTIME_B, C_S, WHITE_KEY },
{31,0,0,0,0,0, BEAT_110, 0, 0, DURATION_EIGHTH, SOLTIME_B, C_E, WHITE_KEY },
{34,0,0,0,0,0, BEAT_110, 0, 0, DURATION_EIGHTH, SOLTIME_B, 0, WHITE_KEY },
```

```
{36,0,0,0,0,0, BEAT_110, 0, 0, DURATION_EIGHTH, SOLTIME_B, 0, WHITE_KEY },
{38,0,0,0,0,0, BEAT_110, 0, 0, DURATION_EIGHTH, SOLTIME_B, 0, WHITE_KEY },
{41,0,0,0,0,0, BEAT_110, 0, 0, DURATION_EIGHTH, SOLTIME_B, 0, WHITE_KEY },
```

//Measure 4 (Repeat)

```
{42,0,0,0,0,0, BEAT_110, 0, 0, DURATION_EIGHTH, SOLTIME_A, C_S, WHITE_KEY },
{24,0,0,0,0,0, BEAT_110, 0, 0, DURATION_EIGHTH, SOLTIME_A, C_E, WHITE_KEY },
{42,0,0,0,0,0, BEAT_110, 0, 0, DURATION_EIGHTH, SOLTIME_B, C_S, WHITE_KEY },
{31,0,0,0,0,0, BEAT_110, 0, 0, DURATION_EIGHTH, SOLTIME_B, C_E, WHITE_KEY },
{0,0,1,1,0,0, BEAT_110, 0, 0, DURATION_EIGHTH, SOLTIME_B, 0, BLACK_KEY },
{38,0,0,0,0,0, BEAT_110, 0, 0, DURATION_EIGHTH, SOLTIME_B, 0, WHITE_KEY },
{0,1,0,0,0,1, BEAT_110, 0, 0, DURATION_EIGHTH, SOLTIME_B, 0, BLACK_KEY },
{42,0,0,0,0,0, BEAT_110, 0, 0, DURATION_EIGHTH, SOLTIME_B, 0, WHITE_KEY },
```

//Measure 5 (Repeat)

```
{43,0,0,0,0,0, BEAT_110, 0, 0, DURATION_EIGHTH, SOLTIME_A, C_S, WHITE_KEY },
{27,0,0,0,0,0, BEAT_110, 0, 0, DURATION_EIGHTH, SOLTIME_A, C_E, WHITE_KEY },
{43,0,0,0,0,0, BEAT_110, 0, 0, DURATION_EIGHTH, SOLTIME_B, C_S WHITE_KEY },
{31,0,0,0,0,0, BEAT_110, 0, 0, DURATION_EIGHTH, SOLTIME_B, C_E, WHITE_KEY },
{34,0,0,0,0,0, BEAT_110, 0, 0, DURATION_EIGHTH, SOLTIME_B, 0, WHITE_KEY },
{38,0,0,0,0,0, BEAT_110, 0, 0, DURATION_EIGHTH, SOLTIME_B, 0, WHITE_KEY },
{45,0,0,0,0,0, BEAT_110, 0, 0, DURATION_EIGHTH, SOLTIME_B, 0, WHITE_KEY },
{0,1,0,1,0,0, BEAT_110, 0, 0, DURATION_EIGHTH, SOLTIME_B, 0, BLACK_KEY },
```

//Measure 6 (Repeat)

```
{45,0,0,0,0,0, BEAT_110, 0, 0, DURATION_EIGHTH, SOLTIME_B, 0, WHITE_KEY },
{0,1,0,1,0,0, BEAT_110, 0, 0, DURATION_EIGHTH, SOLTIME_B, 0, BLACK_KEY },
{45,0,0,0,0,0, BEAT_110, 0, 0, DURATION_EIGHTH, SOLTIME_B, 0, WHITE_KEY },
{42,0,0,0,0,0, BEAT_110, 0, 0, DURATION_EIGHTH, SOLTIME_B, 0, WHITE_KEY },
{44,0,0,0,0,0, BEAT_110, 0, 0, DURATION_EIGHTH, SOLTIME_B, 0, WHITE_KEY },
{43,0,0,0,0,0, BEAT_110, 0, 0, DURATION_EIGHTH, SOLTIME_B, 0, WHITE_KEY },
```

//Measure 7 (Repeat)

```
{41,0,0,0,0,0, BEAT_110, 0, 0, DURATION_EIGHTH, SOLTIME_A, C_S, WHITE_KEY },
{27,0,0,0,0,0, BEAT_110, 0, 0, DURATION_EIGHTH, SOLTIME_A, C_E, WHITE_KEY },
{41,0,0,0,0,0, BEAT_110, 0, 0, DURATION_EIGHTH, SOLTIME_B, C_S, WHITE_KEY },
{31,0,0,0,0,0, BEAT_110, 0, 0, DURATION_EIGHTH, SOLTIME_B, C_E, WHITE_KEY },
{34,0,0,0,0,0, BEAT_110, 0, 0, DURATION_EIGHTH, SOLTIME_B, 0, WHITE_KEY },
{36,0,0,0,0,0, BEAT_110, 0, 0, DURATION_EIGHTH, SOLTIME_B, 0, WHITE_KEY },
{38,0,0,0,0,0, BEAT_110, 0, 0, DURATION_EIGHTH, SOLTIME_B, 0, WHITE_KEY },
{41,0,0,0,0,0, BEAT_110, 0, 0, DURATION_EIGHTH, SOLTIME_B, 0, WHITE_KEY },
```

//Measure 8 (Repeat)

```
{42,0,0,0,0,0, BEAT_110, 0, 0, DURATION_EIGHTH, SOLTIME_A, C_S, WHITE_KEY },
{24,0,0,0,0,0, BEAT_110, 0, 0, DURATION_EIGHTH, SOLTIME_A, C_E, WHITE_KEY },
{42,0,0,0,0,0, BEAT_110, 0, 0, DURATION_EIGHTH, SOLTIME_B, C_SWHITE_KEY },
{31,0,0,0,0,0, BEAT_110, 0, 0, DURATION_EIGHTH, SOLTIME_B, C_E, WHITE_KEY },
{0,0,1,1,0,0, BEAT_110, 0, 0, DURATION_EIGHTH, SOLTIME_B, 0, BLACK_KEY },
{37,0,0,0,0,0, BEAT_110, 0, 0, DURATION_EIGHTH, SOLTIME_B, 0, WHITE_KEY },
{43,0,0,0,0,0, BEAT_110, 0, 0, DURATION_EIGHTH, SOLTIME_B, 0, WHITE_KEY },
{42,0,0,0,0,0, BEAT_110, 0, 0, DURATION_EIGHTH, SOLTIME_B, 0, WHITE_KEY },
```

In the second go-round we skip measure 9 and play measure 10 which is close to our familiar measure 7. Copy and paste measure 7 and modify the ports of the last 3 notes.

//Measure 10

```
{41,0,0,0,0,0, BEAT_110, 0, 0, DURATION_EIGHTH, SOLTIME_A, C_S, WHITE_KEY },
{27,0,0,0,0,0, BEAT_110, 0, 0, DURATION_EIGHTH, SOLTIME_A, C_E, WHITE_KEY },
{41,0,0,0,0,0, BEAT_110, 0, 0, DURATION_EIGHTH, SOLTIME_B, C_S, WHITE_KEY },
{31,0,0,0,0,0, BEAT_110, 0, 0, DURATION_EIGHTH, SOLTIME_B, C_E, WHITE_KEY },
{34,0,0,0,0,0, BEAT_110, 0, 0, DURATION_EIGHTH, SOLTIME_B, 0, WHITE_KEY },
{42,0,0,0,0,0, BEAT_110, 0, 0, DURATION_EIGHTH, SOLTIME_B, 0, WHITE_KEY },
{43,0,0,0,0,0, BEAT_110, 0, 0, DURATION_EIGHTH, SOLTIME_B, 0, WHITE_KEY },
{44,0,0,0,0,0, BEAT_110, 0, 0, DURATION_EIGHTH, SOLTIME_B, 0, WHITE_KEY },
```

In measures 11, 12 and 13, Beethoven throws us another curve by starting the measure with a quarter note with a dot which means that it has a duration equal to three eighth notes. We will code such durations with two eighth notes with 100% soltime and the third as an eighth-note with a 75% soltime. These 3 notes will be paired with the appropriate eighth notes in the bass staff to make three two-note chords. The other three notes in these measures are normal eighth notes. Measure 10 is fairly close, so let's copy and paste it in. To convert measure 10 to measure 11, insert a copy of line 1 after line 4, then correct all nine port numbers and change the soltime to an A in the third line and to a B in the fifth line. We can now copy and paste the re-written measure 11 to code measures 12 and 13. Most port numbers need to be changed but the rest of the lines are correct.

//Measure 11

```
{45,0,0,0,0,0, BEAT_110, 0, 0, DURATION_EIGHTH, SOLTIME_A, C_S, WHITE_KEY },
{29,0,0,0,0,0, BEAT_110, 0, 0, DURATION_EIGHTH, SOLTIME_A, C_E, WHITE_KEY },
{45,0,0,0,0,0, BEAT_110, 0, 0, DURATION_EIGHTH, SOLTIME_A, C_S, WHITE_KEY },
{33,0,0,0,0,0, BEAT_110, 0, 0, DURATION_EIGHTH, SOLTIME_A, C_E, WHITE_KEY },
{45,0,0,0,0,0, BEAT_110, 0, 0, DURATION_EIGHTH, SOLTIME_B, C_S, WHITE_KEY },
{36,0,0,0,0,0, BEAT_110, 0, 0, DURATION_EIGHTH, SOLTIME_B, C_E, WHITE_KEY },
{40,0,0,0,0,0, BEAT_110, 0, 0, DURATION_EIGHTH, SOLTIME_B, 0, WHITE_KEY },
{46,0,0,0,0,0, BEAT_110, 0, 0, DURATION_EIGHTH, SOLTIME_B, 0, WHITE_KEY },
{45,0,0,0,0,0, BEAT_110, 0, 0, DURATION_EIGHTH, SOLTIME_B, 0, WHITE_KEY },
```

//Measure 12

```
{44,0,0,0,0,0, BEAT_110, 0, 0, DURATION_EIGHTH, SOLTIME_A, C_S, WHITE_KEY },
{26,0,0,0,0,0, BEAT_110, 0, 0, DURATION_EIGHTH, SOLTIME_A, C_E, WHITE_KEY },
{44,0,0,0,0,0, BEAT_110, 0, 0, DURATION_EIGHTH, SOLTIME_A, C_S, WHITE_KEY },
{33,0,0,0,0,0, BEAT_110, 0, 0, DURATION_EIGHTH, SOLTIME_A, C_E, WHITE_KEY },
{44,0,0,0,0,0, BEAT_110, 0, 0, DURATION_EIGHTH, SOLTIME_B, C_S, WHITE_KEY },
{35,0,0,0,0,0, BEAT_110, 0, 0, DURATION_EIGHTH, SOLTIME_B, C_E, WHITE_KEY },
{39,0,0,0,0,0, BEAT_110, 0, 0, DURATION_EIGHTH, SOLTIME_B, 0, WHITE_KEY },
{45,0,0,0,0,0, BEAT_110, 0, 0, DURATION_EIGHTH, SOLTIME_B, 0, WHITE_KEY },
{44,0,0,0,0,0, BEAT_110, 0, 0, DURATION_EIGHTH, SOLTIME_B, 0, WHITE_KEY },
```

//Measure 13

```
{43,0,0,0,0,0, BEAT_110, 0, 0, DURATION_EIGHTH, SOLTIME_A, C_S, WHITE_KEY },
{27,0,0,0,0,0, BEAT_110, 0, 0, DURATION_EIGHTH, SOLTIME_A, C_E, WHITE_KEY },
{43,0,0,0,0,0, BEAT_110, 0, 0, DURATION_EIGHTH, SOLTIME_A, C_S, WHITE_KEY },
{31,0,0,0,0,0, BEAT_110, 0, 0, DURATION_EIGHTH, SOLTIME_A, C_E, WHITE_KEY },
{43,0,0,0,0,0, BEAT_110, 0, 0, DURATION_EIGHTH, SOLTIME_B, C_S, WHITE_KEY },
{34,0,0,0,0,0, BEAT_110, 0, 0, DURATION_EIGHTH, SOLTIME_B, C_E, WHITE_KEY },
{38,0,0,0,0,0, BEAT_110, 0, 0, DURATION_EIGHTH, SOLTIME_B, 0, WHITE_KEY },
{43,0,0,0,0,0, BEAT_110, 0, 0, DURATION_EIGHTH, SOLTIME_B, 0, WHITE_KEY },
```

Everything looked normal in measure 14 until the last note which is preceded by (horrors) a treble clef. This means that the notes on the bass staff are played as if they were on the treble staff until we run into a bass clef on the next line which will bring things back to normal. Fortunately, with our mini-robots, we don't have to worry about which hand or finger to use! We will simply code this note, our first eighth note with a tail, as an E (port number 38). Measure 7 is similar to measure 14, so let's copy and paste it one more time. Only the port numbers have to be updated.

//Measure 14

```
{42,0,0,0,0,0, BEAT_110, 0, 0, DURATION_EIGHTH, SOLTIME_A, C_S, WHITE_KEY },
{24,0,0,0,0,0, BEAT_110, 0, 0, DURATION_EIGHTH, SOLTIME_A, C_E, WHITE_KEY },
{42,0,0,0,0,0, BEAT_110, 0, 0, DURATION_EIGHTH, SOLTIME_B, C_S, WHITE_KEY },
{31,0,0,0,0,0, BEAT_110, 0, 0, DURATION_EIGHTH, SOLTIME_B, C_E, WHITE_KEY },
{38,0,0,0,0,0, BEAT_110, 0, 0, DURATION_EIGHTH, SOLTIME_B, 0, WHITE_KEY },
{38,0,0,0,0,0, BEAT_110, 0, 0, DURATION_EIGHTH, SOLTIME_B, 0, WHITE_KEY },
{45,0,0,0,0,0, BEAT_110, 0, 0, DURATION_EIGHTH, SOLTIME_B, 0, WHITE_KEY },
{38,0,0,0,0,0, BEAT_110, 0, 0, DURATION_EIGHTH, SOLTIME_B, 0, WHITE_KEY },
```

In spite of the high-pitched notes and the four accidentals measures 15 and 16 are easy enough to code. There is a close family resemblance to measure 2, so we will copy and paste it in these two measures, correct the port numbers and make sure that the black keys are coded correctly.

//Measure 15

```
{45,0,0,0,0,0, BEAT_110, 0, 0, DURATION_EIGHTH, SOLTIME_B, 0, WHITE_KEY },
{45,0,0,0,0,0, BEAT_110, 0, 0, DURATION_EIGHTH, SOLTIME_B, 0, WHITE_KEY },
{52,0,0,0,0,0, BEAT_110, 0, 0, DURATION_EIGHTH, SOLTIME_B, 0, WHITE_KEY },
{0,1,0,1,0,0, BEAT_110, 0, 0, DURATION_EIGHTH, SOLTIME_B, 0, BLACK_KEY },
{45,0,0,0,0,0, BEAT_110, 0, 0, DURATION_EIGHTH, SOLTIME_B, 0, WHITE_KEY },
{0,1,0,1,0,0, BEAT_110, 0, 0, DURATION_EIGHTH, SOLTIME_B, 0, BLACK_KEY },
```

//Measure 16

```
{45,0,0,0,0,0, BEAT_110, 0, 0, DURATION_EIGHTH, SOLTIME_B, 0, WHITE_KEY },
{0,1,0,1,0,0, BEAT_110, 0, 0, DURATION_EIGHTH, SOLTIME_B, 0, BLACK_KEY },
{45,0,0,0,0,0, BEAT_110, 0, 0, DURATION_EIGHTH, SOLTIME_B, 0, WHITE_KEY },
{0,1,0,1,0,0, BEAT_110, 0, 0, DURATION_EIGHTH, SOLTIME_B, 0, BLACK_KEY },
{44,0,0,0,0,0, BEAT_110, 0, 0, DURATION_EIGHTH, SOLTIME_B, 0, WHITE_KEY },
{43,0,0,0,0,0, BEAT_110, 0, 0, DURATION_EIGHTH, SOLTIME_B, 0, WHITE_KEY },
```

Measures 17, 18, 19 and 20 are exact duplicates of measures 2, 3, 4 and 5. To complete the first page of code of "Fur Elise," it is simply a matter of copying and pasting these four measures as shown below.

//Measure 17

```
{45,0,0,0,0,0, BEAT_110, 0, 0, DURATION_EIGHTH, SOLTIME_B, 0, WHITE_KEY },
{0,1,0,1,0,0, BEAT_110, 0, 0, DURATION_EIGHTH, SOLTIME_B, 0, BLACK_KEY },
{45,0,0,0,0,0, BEAT_110, 0, 0, DURATION_EIGHTH, SOLTIME_B, 0, WHITE_KEY },
{42,0,0,0,0,0, BEAT_110, 0, 0, DURATION_EIGHTH, SOLTIME_B, 0, WHITE_KEY },
{45,0,0,0,0,0, BEAT_110, 0, 0, DURATION_EIGHTH, SOLTIME_B, 0, WHITE_KEY },
{44,0,0,0,0,0, BEAT_110, 0, 0, DURATION_EIGHTH, SOLTIME_B, 0, WHITE_KEY },
```

//Measure 18

```
{41,0,0,0,0,0, BEAT_110, 0, 0, DURATION_EIGHTH, SOLTIME_A, C_S, WHITE_KEY },
{27,0,0,0,0,0, BEAT_110, 0, 0, DURATION_EIGHTH, SOLTIME_A, C_E, WHITE_KEY },
{41,0,0,0,0,0, BEAT_110, 0, 0, DURATION_EIGHTH, SOLTIME_B, C_S, WHITE_KEY },
{31,0,0,0,0,0, BEAT_110, 0, 0, DURATION_EIGHTH, SOLTIME_B, C_E, WHITE_KEY },
{34,0,0,0,0,0, BEAT_110, 0, 0, DURATION_EIGHTH, SOLTIME_B, 0, WHITE_KEY },
{36,0,0,0,0,0, BEAT_110, 0, 0, DURATION_EIGHTH, SOLTIME_B, 0, WHITE_KEY },
{38,0,0,0,0,0, BEAT_110, 0, 0, DURATION_EIGHTH, SOLTIME_B, 0, WHITE_KEY },
{41,0,0,0,0,0, BEAT_110, 0, 0, DURATION_EIGHTH, SOLTIME_B, 0, WHITE_KEY },
```

//Measure 19

```
{42,0,0,0,0,0, BEAT_110, 0, 0, DURATION_EIGHTH, SOLTIME_A, C_S, WHITE_KEY },
{24,0,0,0,0,0, BEAT_110, 0, 0, DURATION_EIGHTH, SOLTIME_A, C_E, WHITE_KEY },
{42,0,0,0,0,0, BEAT_110, 0, 0, DURATION_EIGHTH, SOLTIME_B, C_S, WHITE_KEY },
{31,0,0,0,0,0, BEAT_110, 0, 0, DURATION_EIGHTH, SOLTIME_B, C_E, WHITE_KEY },
{0,0,1,1,0,0, BEAT_110, 0, 0, DURATION_EIGHTH, SOLTIME_B, 0, BLACK_KEY },
{38,0,0,0,0,0, BEAT_110, 0, 0, DURATION_EIGHTH, SOLTIME_B, 0, WHITE_KEY },
{0,1,0,0,0,1, BEAT_110, 0, 0, DURATION_EIGHTH, SOLTIME_B, 0, BLACK_KEY },
{42,0,0,0,0,0, BEAT_110, 0, 0, DURATION_EIGHTH, SOLTIME_B, 0, WHITE_KEY },
```

//Measure 20

```
{43,0,0,0,0,0, BEAT_110, 0, 0, DURATION_EIGHTH, SOLTIME_A, C_S, WHITE_KEY },
{27,0,0,0,0,0, BEAT_110, 0, 0, DURATION_EIGHTH, SOLTIME_A, C_E, WHITE_KEY },
{43,0,0,0,0,0, BEAT_110, 0, 0, DURATION_EIGHTH, SOLTIME_B, C_S, WHITE_KEY },
{31,0,0,0,0,0, BEAT_110, 0, 0, DURATION_EIGHTH, SOLTIME_B, C_E, WHITE_KEY },
{34,0,0,0,0,0, BEAT_110, 0, 0, DURATION_EIGHTH, SOLTIME_B, 0, WHITE_KEY },
{38,0,0,0,0,0, BEAT_110, 0, 0, DURATION_EIGHTH, SOLTIME_B, 0, WHITE_KEY },
{45,0,0,0,0,0, BEAT_110, 0, 0, DURATION_EIGHTH, SOLTIME_B, 0, WHITE_KEY },
{0,1,0,1,0,0, BEAT_110, 0, 0, DURATION_EIGHTH, SOLTIME_B, 0, BLACK_KEY },
```

In Chapter 15 we will use the first eight measures of "Elise" to build our own "Elise" diagnostic sketch. With this diagnostic sketch we will diagnose problems, show oscilloscope images of the operation of the solenoids and provide a vehicle to run the Arduino test program called the "Serial Monitor."

The new symbols that we've encountered while coding "Elise" are: the three symbols for sharp and flat notes, the diminutive clef that shift us to another staff, notes with dots denoting a 50% increase in duration and the double vertical lines that indicate that the preceding measures must be repeated.

One symbol which does not appear until page 2 of "Elise" but that I have seen in other sheet music is a diminutive note symbol. This tells us that it is barely a blip of a note which is not supposed to take any time in the measure (not something that an engineer can understand, but this is art!). Such a fleeting note is coded as a sixteenth note (soltime B) using the special blip note beat of 300. That combination would energize the solenoid for about 35 milliseconds and the next note would start about 15 milliseconds later. We did not run into any ties or slurs but they would be coded by turning on the sustain feature for the notes that are played together. With these new capabilities we can feel confident that we can handle just about anything that the sheet music can throw at us.

Charts for Selecting and Coding the Black and White keys

We have talked about these helpful devices and charts for the coding of the songs before, but let us review them here. First we need the sheet of paper with a two inch cut out to help us focus on the measure that we are coding. Next, we need the chart which we designed for the configuration that we are implementing (see Photo 12.1) mounted on a cardboard stand. It is an extension of the basic 50 note chart shown in Fig 4.2. To code the ports of the black keys in binary, we need the chart in Fig 11.1 to determine the port numbers of the sharps and flats located next to a white key with a known port number. Finally, if necessary, refer to the information in the master charts, such a Fig 7.1 and 7.2, which are the basis for wiring the solenoids.

Summary of Chapter 13

So, there you have it, 28 measures and 200 lines of code. With a little practice, it is not a difficult job and, in this case, not too time consuming due to a great deal of repetition in the music. There are approximately 30 two-note chords which reduce the note playing from 200 to approximately 170 notes. Assuming a beat of 110 BPM, (550 milliseconds per quarter note) and that all notes are eighth notes, the calculated duration of the music on this page is: 170 X 550/ 2 = 46 seconds. The actual time measured with a beat of 110 BPM was clocked at 42 seconds. 1380 bytes are needed to code the 200 notes. At this rate, the 256,000 bytes of storage in the Mega would provide 130 minutes of music.

Of the 200 notes coded, there were 29 unique white notes and three unique black notes. The pitch of the notes on this page ranged from a low E to a high E four octaves higher. The low E is 12 white keys away from middle C while the high E is 16 white keys away from middle C. Many notes between these two extremes are played several times in this and the following pages of the music but the notes just one octave away (seven white keys or 12 white and black keys) on each side of middle C are by far the most common.

CHAPTER 14

The Sketch "Robo"

In Chapter 11 we reviewed the symbols used in sheet music to denote the meaning of the song's notes. We also explained the need for and the meaning of the eight bits of information that need to be coded for each note. We then went through all the preliminary coding needed to define each bit of information properly. In Chapters 12 and 13 we used all this information to code the first page of two songs: "When the Saints Go Marching in" and "Fur Elise." This chapter describes what the operating part of the Robo sketch is expected to do and shows how it does its job of playing each note. We will start with a flow diagram which shows the sequence of the Robo operations.

The long list of "#defines" provided the choices that we have for each note. For instance, we can make the rhythm of the music be fast or slow by selecting a fast beat or a slow beat or we can add "sustain" to the note. Excluding "song end," there are eight groups of "#defines" which are used for each line of code. A typical line of code is shown below; the commas are used to delineate the eight groups.

{36,0,0,0,0,0, BEAT_120, 0, 0, DURATION_QUARTER, SOLTIME_B, 0, WHITE_KEY },

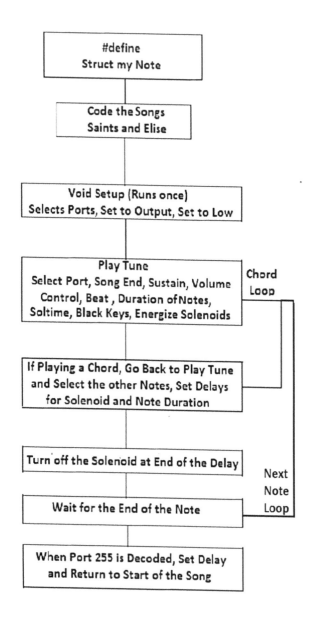

Fig 14.1 – The Robo Flow Diagram

The Robo Flow Diagram

Robo is the name of the sketch that transforms the note data into music. In the Robo flow diagram pictured above, the top two boxes represent the "# defines" notations and the coding of the songs that was done in Chapters 12 and 13. The implementation of the other six boxes is the subject of this chapter. We have work to do!

As we discussed before, there are two commands required in every Arduino sketch: "void setup" and "void loop". We run into the "void setup" command immediately after the "struct my note" command which, with pointer (*), directs us to the song to be played "pSong = Elise." This simply means that we are going to play the notes that we coded from the sheet music for Elise one after the other.

```
struct myNote * pSong = Elise;

void setup()      //the setup routine runs once when the reset switch is pressed
                  //it initializes the digital pins as outputs or inputs
                  //it sets the output of the ports to low (off)

{
pSong = Elise;

int i = START_FIRST_KEY;        // Turn off ports 0-4
while(i <= END_FIRST_KEY) {
pinMode(i, OUTPUT);
digitalWrite(i, LOW);
i++;
      }
i = START_BLACK_KEY;            // Turn off ports 5-9
while(i <= END_BLACK_KEY) {
pinMode(i, OUTPUT);
digitalWrite(i, LOW);
 i++;
  }
i = START_CONFIG_KEY;                    // Turn off ports 10-17
while(i <= END_CONFIG_KEY) {
pinMode(i, OUTPUT);
digitalWrite(i, LOW);
```

```
i++;
    }
i = START_WHITE_KEY;              // Turn off ports 22-53
while(i <= END_WHITE_KEY) {
pinMode(i, OUTPUT);
digitalWrite(i, LOW);
i++;
  }
{
pinMode(18, OUTPUT);              // Select ports 18 and 19
 pinMode(19, OUTPUT);
  }
}
```

As the "//comments" above and the words in the flow chart box tell us, the "void setup" code selects the white and black ports, initializes them to be output ports (there are no input ports in this sketch) and then sets them to low (turns them off). We have mentioned that when power is first turned on, the Mega's port can float between on and off; this code makes sure that they are selected as outputs and turned off at the start of the song.

To "#define" the ports and select them in the Robo sketch, we must make a decision about the configuration that we want to implement. We have talked about a 50-key configuration which matches the four-octave range of the guitar, is suitable for pop music and is the easiest and the least expensive to implement. We have also shown a configuration that activates all 76 keys of the keyboard and the in-between 60-key configuration that we are implementing here. Obviously, the Robo sketch must reflect the configuration that has been chosen.

If the grouping of ports seems odd, remember that we count keys from each side of middle C. The ports 5 to 9 needed to be together to generate the binary code. We also tried to keep the large group of ports in the end connector (ports 20 to 53) together for ease of wiring. I will grant that it could have been done differently, possibly in a simpler way.

Play a Tune

After all this preparation we are finally ready to play a tune, which means selecting the correct mini-robot and activating it for the correct amount of time. If the note in question is part of a chord, we will select the other notes in the chord. If not we will move on to the next note. All this preparation work only took the Mega a few millionths of a second to perform and is completely undetectable.

"void playTune" is the instruction (command) which tells Robo to look at the line of code that we wrote for the first note. According to the structure of the note's line of code (struct myNote * pTune) we will proceed to the selection of the note's port (before the first comma). We have to be careful here, as a zero does not mean that we do not have a white note because there actually is a port 0. We will use the words "BLACK_KEY" to establish that the following five binary bits select a black port. The Robo code starting with "void playTune" is shown below.

```
void playTune(struct myNote * pTune) {

byte Port1 = pTune->Port;        // Select a Port
int Soltime= pTune->Soltime;     // Select one of 4 setting for the solenoid
                                 // time duration
if(Port1 == SONG_END) {          // End the song when Port 255 is detected
pSong = pTune;
return;

}
if(pTune->Sustain == 1) {        // Turn on the sustain feature on Port 18
digitalWrite(18, HIGH);

}
if(pTune->Sustain == 0) {        //Turn off the sustain feature on Port 18
digitalWrite(18, LOW);

}
if(pTune->Volume == 1) {         //Turn the volume feature to low on Port 19
digitalWrite(19, HIGH);

}
```

```
if(pTune->Volume == 0) {        //Turn the volume feature to full on Port 19
digitalWrite(19, LOW);

}

int beat = pTune->Beat ;     // Establish the beat time of the song (millisecs)
beat = beat * beatMult[pTune->Duration]/4;   //Calculate the duration time
                                          // of the note in milliseconds
int durMS = beat * Soltime/4; // Calculate the duration time of the solenoids
```

Port1 is the byte of data containing the port number of a white key as pointed to by the expression "pTune->Port"

Soltime is an integer (a whole number) to be inserted in the formula that determines the amount of time that the key/solenoid is activated. It is pointed to by the expression "pTune->Soltime"

Next, we check to see whether we have reached SONG_END. If port 255 is detected, that means that we have reached the last note of the song and we must re-start the song at the beginning after a five second delay.

We then check to see which way the toggle of sustain is set. When the pointer to the expression "pTune->Sustain==1" tells us that sustain is to be turned on, we will activate port 18 with a "digital-Write(18, HIGH)". In other words, if sustain is to be turned on, port 18 will be set to high. The next action is to check if sustain needs to be turned off using a Sustain==0. If that is the case a digitalWrite(18, LOW) will be executed.

The same thing is done with Volume in the next four lines of code. A "1" will turn the volume down with digitalWrite(19, HIGH) and a "0" will turn the volume back to normal with a digitalWrite(19 LOW).

The next pointer establishes an integer for the duration of the "Beat" in millisecs (ms) by referring to the #define table of beats which range from 60 to 300 beats per minute. For instance, a BEAT_120 will have a duration of 500ms.

The beat duration of a note depends on the type of note that we are playing. For instance, a full note will have a beat duration four times as long as that of a quarter note. The next line of code is a formula: beat = beat * beat Mult[pTune->Duration]/4. It determines the note's duration by multiplying the beat by the beat multiplier and dividing by 4. For example, when the beat of the song is 120 BPM and the quarter note has the beat, a short one sixteenth note will last: 500ms times 1 (multiplier for a sixteenth note) divided by 4 or 125ms.

The next line of Robo code tells us the duration of the solenoid operation as a percentage of the beat of the note. Four different percentages can be coded: A = 100%, B =75% (normal setting), C = 50% and D = 25%. In the example cited above, the solenoid for the sixteenth note would be energized for 62ms if the soltime is a C. The code that performs this calculation is the formula: int durMS = beat * Soltime/4. "int durMS" means that the duration of the solenoid closure is an integer which is equal to the beat of the note multiplied by the soltime divided by 4. Its range is equal to the beat (100%=A) down to one quarter of the beat of the note (25%=D).

Notice that both equations are divided by four. We did that to avoid decimals which take a long time to calculate. For instance, instead of using a .25 for 25%, we used a 1 and then divided the whole equation by the integer 4.

The last item to describe from this box in the flow chart shows how to select the port that activates the black keys—if we point to the last bit of data in the line of code and find the words BLACK_KEY. That means that we have to decode the address of the solenoid for this black key. It is easier than it sounds. Let's paste in the code and analyze it.

```
if(pTune->BlackKey == HIGH) {
    digitalWrite(5, pTune->blackStateP5);
    digitalWrite(6, pTune->blackStateP6);
    digitalWrite(7, pTune->blackStateP7);
    digitalWrite(8, pTune->blackStateP8);
    digitalWrite(9, pTune->blackStateP9);
```

```
} else {
   if(Port1) {
      digitalWrite(Port1, HIGH);    // Execute command HIGH for the designated
                                    // white or black note
   }                                // Energize the solenoids for duration durMs
}
```

The "if" command tells us to perform a certain action if we find the words "BLACK_KEY" in the line of code for the notes and a different action if we do not. If we find "BLACK_KEY", we will "digitalWrite" (activate) ports 5 through 9 according to the "1" or "0" of blackState P5 through P9. In other words, we will activate the five ports with a binary number in the five spaces separated by commas right after the port number of the white key according to the 1's and 0's that we find in P5 to P9.

If it is not a black key, the command will drop us down to "else" in which case we will "digitalWrite" (activate) the value of Port1 which is the port number of the white key. That concludes processing the information in the line of code for the first note. Next, we will deal with the chords.

Playing a Chord

When a chord is to be played, at least two notes are coded: the START note and the END note. For chords with more than two notes any number of CONTINUE notes can be inserted between the start and end notes. Since they are all played at the same time, they can be listed in any order. The Soltime of the "END" note controls the time interval before the solenoids/keys are released. All notes in the chord have the same beat duration. For instance, they might all be quarter notes. The Robo code to play chords is shown below.

```
if((pChordTune->Chord == CHORD_START) || (pChordTune->Chord == CHORD_CONTINUE)) {
    pChordTune++;                 // Combine individual notes into chords
    playTune(pChordTune);
    }

    if((pTune->Chord == CHORD_END) || (pTune->Chord == 0)) {
    delay (durMS);                // Determines the length of time that the
    }                             // solenoid is energized. One delay per chord
```

This part of the Robo code also starts with an "if" command. The pointer selects a chord, and if we have a CHORD_START or a CHORD_CONTINUE (the vertical bars "||" denotes an OR function) we will perform the next two lines of code shown between the curly braces (otherwise, we will go to the next "if" command). The first of the two lines of code tell us to add one (++) to chordTune to select the next note and to start at "void playTune". Again, this is the "chord loop" shown on the flow chart.

After having looped through this code as many times as it takes to get to "CHORD_END", we drop down to the next command which starts the durMS delay. The calculation for this delay was described above. Note that CHORD_END and chord==0 (which means that the note is not part of a chord) perform the same function: they start the durMS delay. That is the reason why they are also separated by an OR function (||).

Turning off the Solenoids

The Robo code described above selected and activated the appropriate key/solenoid (several times in the case of a chord). The last line of code started the durMS delay which determines how long the solenoid is activated. It could last as little as 500ms divided by 4 multiplied by 25 % (or 31ms), for a sixteenth-note with a soltime of D

or as long as two seconds for a full note with a soltime of A. When
this delay ends, we use the code shown below to tell the solenoid(s)
to release the key(s).

```
if(pTune->BlackKey == HIGH) {        //Turn off the black keys (ports 5 to 9)
int i = START_BLACK_KEY;             // after the end of the durMS delay
while(i <= END_BLACK_KEY) {
pinMode(i, OUTPUT);
digitalWrite(i, LOW);
  i++;
    }
}else {
int i = START_FIRST_KEY;             //Turn off the white keys (ports 0 to 4)
while(i <= END_FIRST_KEY) {          // after the end of the durMS delay
pinMode(i, OUTPUT);
digitalWrite(i, LOW);
i++;
 }
i = START_CONFIG_KEY;                //Turn off the white keys (ports 10 to 17)
while(i <= END_CONFIG_KEY) {         // after the end of the durMS delay
pinMode(i, OUTPUT);
digitalWrite(i, LOW);
i++;
 }
i = START_WHITE_KEY;                 //Turn off the white keys (ports 20 to 53)
while(i <= END_WHITE_KEY) {          // after the end of the durMS delay

pinMode(i, OUTPUT);
digitalWrite(i, LOW);
i++;
```

It would get pretty messy to attempt to determine which keys were
activated (especially dealing with chords) so the easy solution is to
turn off ALL the solenoids even the ones that were not activated. It
does no harm and it guarantees that all solenoids are reset for the
next note or chord. The code is simple, we select all ports one after
the other and turn them off with a digitalWrite (Low) command.

Turning off the Note or Chord or Start a New One

At this point, we still have to wait for the end of the note because it is likely to last longer than the soltime of the solenoid. Only then can we call out another note. The code is shown below.

```
// Now wait out the beat time (Duration of the note)
if((pTune->Chord == CHORD_END) || (pTune->Chord == 0)) {
pTune++;
pSong = pTune;
delay (beat-durMS);        //After the delay (completion of the note or chord),
                           // select the next note
```

We go back to the "if" command which turned on the solenoid delay "durMS". At this point in the Robo code, the delay has elapsed but the note's beat usually lasts longer than the duration of the solenoid (soltime). To deal with this, we will add another short delay: beat minus durMS which will get us to the end of the note or chord and allow us to play another note.

Void Loop

At long last, we get to the second required command in a sketch: the loop command. Here, the loop routine is used play the next note or replay the entire song or move on to the next song. The code is shown below.

```
void loop()        // the loop routine runs over and over
{
if(pSong->Port == SONG_END)
pSong = Elise;
delay(5000);
}
playTune(pSong);
}
```

The first command is another "if" command. It points to the port of the note to find out if it is equal to SONG_END which will happen if the port number is equal to 255. If it is, we have reached the end of the song "Elise." After a 5 second delay, we will play "Elise" again from the beginning. If not, we will skip the replay and, by going to "playTune", direct the sketch to play the next note or chord of the song in progress. As we will see in Chapter 16 this entire loop operation takes about .4 milliseconds.

Summary of Chapter 14

This chapter defines the composition of the notes and chords and describes how they are played. It should give the reader a good appreciation for the enormous amount of work involved to perform the relatively simple task of activating a solenoid under computer control.

A flow diagram shows the sequence of the actions needed to play a note. Each action is performed so quickly by the Mega compared to the amount of time that it takes to play even the shortest note that the execution of its many commands and the numerous iterations necessary to play chords go completely unnoticed.

After the completion of setup, we play a note by selecting its port number and activating its solenoid. Its time duration is commensurate with the type of note—from full note to one sixteenth note. While the solenoids are usually activated for 75% of the beat time of the note, they can be activated for three other duration periods. The process of selecting the port of a black note is somewhat more difficult due to the nature of its binary encoding process (in a 50-note configuration, there is a port for each black note—consequently, this additional coding is not necessary, but it does no harm to leave it in).

The process of playing chords is also described. It involves interpreting the START, CONTINUE and END characteristics of the notes as shown in their code. Several iterations of the program (one for each note) are needed to play a chord.

Finally, we perform the last needed function of an Arduino sketch, void Loop. This function is used to return to the start of the song, move onto the next song, or to play the next note or chord by decoding the "end of song" port 255 and taking the appropriate action.

Chapter 15 will use this Robo code as the basis for the music sketches and for a diagnostic program to check all the features of the program using the "Serial Monitor". This is a short routine that can be inserted in various locations in the sketch to determine, for instance, if the delays are correct for different types of notes. The very simple diagnostic sketch 5 Sol, which we developed from the basic sketch "blink," is very useful to check the operation of the solenoids in groups of five. But at this point, we need something more extensive to make sure that the rendition of the song is correct.

CHAPTER 15

Diagnostic and Music Sketches

Robo Sketches

The two music sketches and the diagnostic sketch based on the "Robo" platform are very similar: only the code for the music is different. I call the music sketches "MPP Saints from Book 2.0" and "MPP Elise from Book 2.0". Basically, they are identical to the diagnostic sketch which we discuss at length below except that the music code from Chapters 12 and 13 replaces the music code of diagnostic sketch namely: the scales, the 20 combinations and the shortened versions of the two songs. The sketch building of these two music sketches is identical to the sketch building of MPP Elise Diagnostic 10.0 described below.

Diagnostic Methods

The diagnostic sketch that we have developed using Robo as the platform will perform a comprehensive test of all the notes and features of the Robo sketch. Unlike the 5 Sol diagnostic program which was based on the simple "Blink" sketch and was specifically designed to test the operation of the solenoids, MPP Elise Diagnostic 10.0 will exercise all the features of Robo such as chords and sustain. Using this sketch in Chapter 16, we will describe three methods of checking the operation of the Robo sketch: slowing the pace of the music, inserting software that is capable of reporting on the requested data and using routines suitable for the use of an oscilloscope.

Fortunately, because playing the notes is such a slow process (compared to the speed of electronics), the first and simplest way to check the notes in a song is to slow down the tempo and assess what is happening in slow motion. The second method consists of inserting a routine in the Robo sketch that opens the Arduino IDE's "Serial Monitor." With it, it is possible to "print" (display on your PC) the values of certain variables such as the duration of delays like "beat" or "durMS". The third method uses the diagnostic sketch described here to generate two oscilloscope images that the geeks in the audience might enjoy. These three diagnostic methods will be discussed in Chapter 16.

Getting back to building the diagnostic sketch, our first task is to assemble a complete version of the Robo sketch described in Chapter 14 to be used as the platform for this diagnostic sketch. For the music, we will play the scales of the white and black keys, the 20 combinations of note and solenoid durations, as well as the first eight measures of Elise and the first four measures of Saints. By running the entire sketch or a portion of it, it is possible to activate every feature of the player piano.

The musical scales simply start with the first white key and ascend to the forty-fifth white key. Similarly, we will start with the first black key and ascend to the thirty-first black key. This will provide a quick check of all the solenoids and keys. The other Robo features, namely the 20 combinations of note durations and the sustain and volume features, are also tested and described below. To avoid possible errors, there are no abbreviations in the coding of the notes in the sketch below. We will call this sketch "MPP Elise Diagnostic 10.0" and file the sketch under that name.

Note that for configurations having less than 76 keys, the unused lines of code for the unused keys can to be commented out with double slashes (//) or simply left in place knowing that they will not be activated. Notice also that the beat for the two scales and the two songs are different, ranging from 90 to 120. The idea is to be able to change the beat of one section of the diagnostic without affecting the entire sketch. Notice also the following oddity: in the 76-key configuration, white key number one is activated with port 20 (key number one is not active in the 50- or 60-key configuration). We made this change in order to use a series of six zeros separated with commas to indicate a pause. The words WHITE_KEY OR BLACK_KEY have no effect on the coding of a pause.

MPP Elise Diagnostic 10.0

// Start of MPP Elise Diagnostic 10.0

```
#define BEAT_60 999        //Number of ms for various beats as computed
#define BEAT_70 857        // using a metronome's "beats per minute"
#define BEAT_80 750
#define BEAT_90 666
#define BEAT_100 600
#define BEAT_110 550
#define BEAT_120 500
#define BEAT_130 467
#define BEAT_140 433
#define BEAT_150 400
#define BEAT_160 375
#define BEAT_170 352
#define BEAT_180 333
#define BEAT_300 200

#define DURATION_FULL 1        //The time duration in milliseconds is calculated
#define DURATION_HALF 2        //for various types of notes as defined by the
#define DURATION_QUARTER 3     //sheet music and the beat of the music
#define DURATION_EIGHTH 4
#define DURATION_SIXTEENTH 5

#define SOLTIME_A 4        //Solenoid stays energized for 100% of the duration of the note
#define SOLTIME_B 3        //Solenoid stays energized for 75% of the duration of the note
#define SOLTIME_C 2        //Solenoid stays energized for 50% of the duration of the note
```

```
#define SOLTIME_D  1          //Solenoid stays energized for 25% of the duration of the note

#define SUSTAIN_ON 1          //Defines the operation of sustain
#define SUSTAIN_OFF 0

#define VOLUME_LOW 1          //Defines the operation of the volume control
#define VOLUME_FULL 0

#define CHORD_START 1         //Defines chord start, continue (if more than 2 notes) and end
#define CHORD_CONTINUE 2
#define CHORD_END 3

#define WHITE_KEY 0
#define BLACK_KEY 1

#define START_FIRST_KEY 0     //Port numbers for the white and black keys grouped
#define END_FIRST_KEY 4       // according to various configurations

#define START_BLACK_KEY 5
#define END_BLACK_KEY 9

#define START_CONFIG_KEY 10
#define END_CONFIG_KEY 17

#define START_WHITE_KEY 20
#define END_WHITE_KEY 53

#define SONG_END 255

static int beatMult [] = {0,16,8,4,2,1};    //Multiplier used for the duration of the 5 types of notes

struct myNote                 //Structuring of the notes and bit assignment
{
  byte Port;
  byte blackStateP5: 1;
  byte blackStateP6: 1;
  byte blackStateP7: 1;
  byte blackStateP8: 1;
  byte blackStateP9: 1;
  int  Beat;
  byte Sustain :   2;
```

```
    byte Volume :    2;
    byte Duration:   4;
    byte Soltime:    4;
    byte Chord :     4;
    byte BlackKey :  4;

} Note;

struct myNote Elise[] = {

//Scales for the white keys in groups of ten

{20,0,0,0,0,0, BEAT_90, 0, 0, DURATION_EIGHTH, SOLTIME_B, 0, WHITE_KEY },
{1,0,0,0,0,0, BEAT_90, 0, 0, DURATION_EIGHTH, SOLTIME_B, 0, WHITE_KEY },
{2,0,0,0,0,0, BEAT_90, 0, 0, DURATION_EIGHTH, SOLTIME_B, 0, WHITE_KEY },
{3,0,0,0,0,0, BEAT_90, 0, 0, DURATION_EIGHTH, SOLTIME_B, 0, WHITE_KEY },
{4,0,0,0,0,0, BEAT_90, 0, 0, DURATION_EIGHTH, SOLTIME_B, 0, WHITE_KEY },
{22,0,0,0,0,0, BEAT_90, 0, 0, DURATION_EIGHTH, SOLTIME_B, 0, WHITE_KEY },
{23,0,0,0,0,0, BEAT_90, 0, 0, DURATION_EIGHTH, SOLTIME_B, 0, WHITE_KEY },
{24,0,0,0,0,0, BEAT_90, 0, 0, DURATION_EIGHTH, SOLTIME_B, 0, WHITE_KEY },
{25,0,0,0,0,0, BEAT_90, 0, 0, DURATION_EIGHTH, SOLTIME_B, 0, WHITE_KEY },
{26,0,0,0,0,0, BEAT_90, 0, 0, DURATION_EIGHTH, SOLTIME_B, 0, WHITE_KEY },


{27,0,0,0,0,0, BEAT_90, 0, 0, DURATION_EIGHTH, SOLTIME_B, 0, WHITE_KEY },
{28,0,0,0,0,0, BEAT_90, 0, 0, DURATION_EIGHTH, SOLTIME_B, 0, WHITE_KEY },
{29,0,0,0,0,0, BEAT_90, 0, 0, DURATION_EIGHTH, SOLTIME_B, 0, WHITE_KEY },
{30,0,0,0,0,0, BEAT_90, 0, 0, DURATION_EIGHTH, SOLTIME_B, 0, WHITE_KEY },
{31,0,0,0,0,0, BEAT_90, 0, 0, DURATION_EIGHTH, SOLTIME_B, 0, WHITE_KEY },
{32,0,0,0,0,0, BEAT_90, 0, 0, DURATION_EIGHTH, SOLTIME_B, 0, WHITE_KEY },
{33,0,0,0,0,0, BEAT_90, 0, 0, DURATION_EIGHTH, SOLTIME_B, 0, WHITE_KEY },
{34,0,0,0,0,0, BEAT_90, 0, 0, DURATION_EIGHTH, SOLTIME_B, 0, WHITE_KEY },
{35,0,0,0,0,0, BEAT_90, 0, 0, DURATION_EIGHTH, SOLTIME_B, 0, WHITE_KEY },
{36,0,0,0,0,0, BEAT_90, 0, 0, DURATION_EIGHTH, SOLTIME_B, 0, WHITE_KEY },  //mid C

{37,0,0,0,0,0, BEAT_90, 0, 0, DURATION_EIGHTH, SOLTIME_B, 0, WHITE_KEY },
{38,0,0,0,0,0, BEAT_90, 0, 0, DURATION_EIGHTH, SOLTIME_B, 0, WHITE_KEY },
{39,0,0,0,0,0, BEAT_90, 0, 0, DURATION_EIGHTH, SOLTIME_B, 0, WHITE_KEY },
{40,0,0,0,0,0, BEAT_90, 0, 0, DURATION_EIGHTH, SOLTIME_B, 0, WHITE_KEY },
{41,0,0,0,0,0, BEAT_90, 0, 0, DURATION_EIGHTH, SOLTIME_B, 0, WHITE_KEY },
{42,0,0,0,0,0, BEAT_90, 0, 0, DURATION_EIGHTH, SOLTIME_B, 0, WHITE_KEY },
{43,0,0,0,0,0, BEAT_90, 0, 0, DURATION_EIGHTH, SOLTIME_B, 0, WHITE_KEY },
```

{44,0,0,0,0,0, BEAT_90, 0, 0, DURATION_EIGHTH, SOLTIME_B, 0, WHITE_KEY },
{45,0,0,0,0,0, BEAT_90, 0, 0, DURATION_EIGHTH, SOLTIME_B, 0, WHITE_KEY },
{46,0,0,0,0,0, BEAT_90, 0, 0, DURATION_EIGHTH, SOLTIME_B, 0, WHITE_KEY },

{47,0,0,0,0,0, BEAT_90, 0, 0, DURATION_EIGHTH, SOLTIME_B, 0, WHITE_KEY },
{48,0,0,0,0,0, BEAT_90, 0, 0, DURATION_EIGHTH, SOLTIME_B, 0, WHITE_KEY },
{49,0,0,0,0,0, BEAT_90, 0, 0, DURATION_EIGHTH, SOLTIME_B, 0, WHITE_KEY },
{50,0,0,0,0,0, BEAT_90, 0, 0, DURATION_EIGHTH, SOLTIME_B, 0, WHITE_KEY },
{51,0,0,0,0,0, BEAT_90, 0, 0, DURATION_EIGHTH, SOLTIME_B, 0, WHITE_KEY },
{52,0,0,0,0,0, BEAT_90, 0, 0, DURATION_EIGHTH, SOLTIME_B, 0, WHITE_KEY },
{53,0,0,0,0,0, BEAT_90, 0, 0, DURATION_EIGHTH, SOLTIME_B, 0, WHITE_KEY },
{10,0,0,0,0,0, BEAT_90, 0, 0, DURATION_EIGHTH, SOLTIME_B, 0, WHITE_KEY },
{11,0,0,0,0,0, BEAT_90, 0, 0, DURATION_EIGHTH, SOLTIME_B, 0, WHITE_KEY },
{12,0,0,0,0,0, BEAT_90, 0, 0, DURATION_EIGHTH, SOLTIME_B, 0, WHITE_KEY },

{13,0,0,0,0,0, BEAT_90, 0, 0, DURATION_EIGHTH, SOLTIME_B, 0, WHITE_KEY },
{14,0,0,0,0,0, BEAT_90, 0, 0, DURATION_EIGHTH, SOLTIME_B, 0, WHITE_KEY },
{15,0,0,0,0,0, BEAT_90, 0, 0, DURATION_EIGHTH, SOLTIME_B, 0, WHITE_KEY },
{16,0,0,0,0,0, BEAT_90, 0, 0, DURATION_EIGHTH, SOLTIME_B, 0, WHITE_KEY },
{17,0,0,0,0,0, BEAT_90, 0, 0, DURATION_EIGHTH, SOLTIME_B, 0, WHITE_KEY },

//Scales for the black keys in groups of ten

{0,0,0,0,0,1, BEAT_100, 0, 0, DURATION_EIGHTH, SOLTIME_B, 0, BLACK_KEY },
{0,0,0,0,1,0, BEAT_100, 0, 0, DURATION_EIGHTH, SOLTIME_B, 0, BLACK_KEY },
{0,0,0,0,1,1, BEAT_100, 0, 0, DURATION_EIGHTH, SOLTIME_B, 0, BLACK_KEY },
{0,0,0,1,0,0, BEAT_100, 0, 0, DURATION_EIGHTH, SOLTIME_B, 0, BLACK_KEY },
{0,0,0,1,0,1, BEAT_100, 0, 0, DURATION_EIGHTH, SOLTIME_B, 0, BLACK_KEY },
{0,0,0,1,1,0, BEAT_100, 0, 0, DURATION_EIGHTH, SOLTIME_B, 0, BLACK_KEY },
{0,0,0,1,1,1, BEAT_100, 0, 0, DURATION_EIGHTH, SOLTIME_B, 0, BLACK_KEY },
{0,0,1,0,0,0, BEAT_100, 0, 0, DURATION_EIGHTH, SOLTIME_B, 0, BLACK_KEY },
{0,0,1,0,0,1, BEAT_100, 0, 0, DURATION_EIGHTH, SOLTIME_B, 0, BLACK_KEY },
{0,0,1,0,1,0, BEAT_100, 0, 0, DURATION_EIGHTH, SOLTIME_B, 0, BLACK_KEY },

{0,0,1,0,1,1, BEAT_100, 0, 0, DURATION_EIGHTH, SOLTIME_B, 0, BLACK_KEY },
{0,0,1,1,0,0, BEAT_100, 0, 0, DURATION_EIGHTH, SOLTIME_B, 0, BLACK_KEY },
{0,0,1,1,0,1, BEAT_100, 0, 0, DURATION_EIGHTH, SOLTIME_B, 0, BLACK_KEY },
{0,0,1,1,1,0, BEAT_100, 0, 0, DURATION_EIGHTH, SOLTIME_B, 0, BLACK_KEY },
{0,0,1,1,1,1, BEAT_100, 0, 0, DURATION_EIGHTH, SOLTIME_B, 0, BLACK_KEY },
{0,1,0,0,0,0, BEAT_100, 0, 0, DURATION_EIGHTH, SOLTIME_B, 0, BLACK_KEY },
{0,1,0,0,0,1, BEAT_100, 0, 0, DURATION_EIGHTH, SOLTIME_B, 0, BLACK_KEY },

```
{0,1,0,0,1,0, BEAT_100, 0, 0, DURATION_EIGHTH, SOLTIME_B, 0, BLACK_KEY },
{0,1,0,0,1,1, BEAT_100, 0, 0, DURATION_EIGHTH, SOLTIME_B, 0, BLACK_KEY },
{0,1,0,1,0,0, BEAT_100, 0, 0, DURATION_EIGHTH, SOLTIME_B, 0, BLACK_KEY },

{0,1,0,1,0,1, BEAT_100, 0, 0, DURATION_EIGHTH, SOLTIME_B, 0, BLACK_KEY },
{0,1,0,1,1,0, BEAT_100, 0, 0, DURATION_EIGHTH, SOLTIME_B, 0, BLACK_KEY },
{0,1,0,1,1,1, BEAT_100, 0, 0, DURATION_EIGHTH, SOLTIME_B, 0, BLACK_KEY },
{0,1,1,0,0,0, BEAT_100, 0, 0, DURATION_EIGHTH, SOLTIME_B, 0, BLACK_KEY },
{0,1,1,0,0,1, BEAT_100, 0, 0, DURATION_EIGHTH, SOLTIME_B, 0, BLACK_KEY },
{0,1,1,0,1,0, BEAT_100, 0, 0, DURATION_EIGHTH, SOLTIME_B, 0, BLACK_KEY },
{0,1,1,0,1,1, BEAT_100, 0, 0, DURATION_EIGHTH, SOLTIME_B, 0, BLACK_KEY },
{0,1,1,1,0,0, BEAT_100, 0, 0, DURATION_EIGHTH, SOLTIME_B, 0, BLACK_KEY },
{0,1,1,1,0,1, BEAT_100, 0, 0, DURATION_EIGHTH, SOLTIME_B, 0, BLACK_KEY },
{0,1,1,1,1,0, BEAT_100, 0, 0, DURATION_EIGHTH, SOLTIME_B, 0, BLACK_KEY },
{0,1,1,1,1,1, BEAT_100, 0, 0, DURATION_EIGHTH, SOLTIME_B, 0, BLACK_KEY },

// 20 combinations (plus blip) of the duration of the note and the soltime for five ports (36 to 40)

{36,0,0,0,0,0, BEAT_120, 0, 0, DURATION_FULL, SOLTIME_A, 0, WHITE_KEY },
{0,0,0,0,0,0, BEAT_120, 0, 0, DURATION_EIGHTH, SOLTIME_B, 0, WHITE_KEY },
{36,0,0,0,0,0, BEAT_120, 0, 0, DURATION_FULL, SOLTIME_B, 0, WHITE_KEY },
{36,0,0,0,0,0, BEAT_120, 0, 0, DURATION_FULL, SOLTIME_C, 0, WHITE_KEY },
{36,0,0,0,0,0, BEAT_120, 0, 0, DURATION_FULL, SOLTIME_D, 0, WHITE_KEY },

{37,0,0,0,0,0, BEAT_120, 0, 0, DURATION_HALF, SOLTIME_A, 0, WHITE_KEY },
{0,0,0,0,0,0, BEAT_120, 0, 0, DURATION_EIGHTH, SOLTIME_B, 0, WHITE_KEY },
{37,0,0,0,0,0, BEAT_120, 0, 0, DURATION_HALF, SOLTIME_B, 0, WHITE_KEY },
{37,0,0,0,0,0, BEAT_120, 0, 0, DURATION_HALF, SOLTIME_C, 0, WHITE_KEY },
{37,0,0,0,0,0, BEAT_120, 0, 0, DURATION_HALF, SOLTIME_D, 0, WHITE_KEY },

{38,0,0,0,0,0, BEAT_120, 0, 0, DURATION_QUARTER, SOLTIME_A, 0, WHITE_KEY },
{0,0,0,0,0,0, BEAT_120, 0, 0, DURATION_EIGHTH, SOLTIME_B, 0, WHITE_KEY },
{38,0,0,0,0,0, BEAT_120, 0, 0, DURATION_QUARTER, SOLTIME_B, 0, WHITE_KEY },
{38,0,0,0,0,0, BEAT_120, 0, 0, DURATION_QUARTER, SOLTIME_C, 0, WHITE_KEY },
{38,0,0,0,0,0, BEAT_120, 0, 0, DURATION_QUARTER, SOLTIME_D, 0, WHITE_KEY },

{39,0,0,0,0,0, BEAT_120, 0, 0, DURATION_EIGHTH, SOLTIME_A, 0, WHITE_KEY },
{0,0,0,0,0,0, BEAT_120, 0, 0, DURATION_EIGHTH, SOLTIME_B, 0, WHITE_KEY },
{39,0,0,0,0,0, BEAT_120, 0, 0, DURATION_EIGHTH, SOLTIME_B, 0, WHITE_KEY },
{39,0,0,0,0,0, BEAT_120, 0, 0, DURATION_EIGHTH, SOLTIME_C, 0, WHITE_KEY },
```

{39,0,0,0,0,0, BEAT_120, 0, 0, DURATION_EIGHTH, SOLTIME_D, 0, WHITE_KEY },

{40,0,0,0,0,0, BEAT_120, 0, 0, DURATION_SIXTEENTH, SOLTIME_A, 0, WHITE_KEY },
{0,0,0,0,0,0, BEAT_120, 0, 0, DURATION_EIGHTH, SOLTIME_B, 0, WHITE_KEY },
{40,0,0,0,0,0, BEAT_120, 0, 0, DURATION_SIXTEENTH, SOLTIME_B, 0, WHITE_KEY },
{40,0,0,0,0,0, BEAT_120, 0, 0, DURATION_SIXTEENTH, SOLTIME_C, 0, WHITE_KEY },
{40,0,0,0,0,0, BEAT_120, 0, 0, DURATION_SIXTEENTH, SOLTIME_D, 0, WHITE_KEY },

{0,0,0,0,0,0, BEAT_120, 0, 0, DURATION_SIXTEENTH, SOLTIME_B, 0, WHITE_KEY },
{0,0,0,0,0,0, BEAT_120, 0, 0, DURATION_SIXTEENTH, SOLTIME_B, 0, WHITE_KEY },
{41,0,0,0,0,0, BEAT_300, 0, 0, DURATION_SIXTEENTH, SOLTIME_B, 0, WHITE_KEY },

//Coding of the first eight measures of Elise

//Measure 1
{45,0,0,0,0,0, BEAT_110, 0, 0, DURATION_EIGHTH, SOLTIME_B, 0, WHITE_KEY },
{0,1,0,1,0,0, BEAT_110, 0, 0, DURATION_EIGHTH, SOLTIME_B, 0, BLACK_KEY },

//Measure 2
{45,0,0,0,0,0, BEAT_110, 0, 0, DURATION_EIGHTH, SOLTIME_B, 0, WHITE_KEY },
{0,1,0,1,0,0, BEAT_110, 0, 0, DURATION_EIGHTH, SOLTIME_B, 0, BLACK_KEY },
{45,0,0,0,0,0, BEAT_110, 0, 0, DURATION_EIGHTH, SOLTIME_B, 0, WHITE_KEY },
{42,0,0,0,0,0, BEAT_110, 0, 0, DURATION_EIGHTH, SOLTIME_B, 0, WHITE_KEY },
{44,0,0,0,0,0, BEAT_110, 0, 0, DURATION_EIGHTH, SOLTIME_B, 0, WHITE_KEY },
{43,0,0,0,0,0, BEAT_110, 0, 0, DURATION_EIGHTH, SOLTIME_B, 0, WHITE_KEY },

//Measure 3
{41,0,0,0,0,0, BEAT_110, 0, 0, DURATION_EIGHTH, SOLTIME_A, CHORD_START, WHITE_KEY },
{27,0,0,0,0,0, BEAT_110, 0, 0, DURATION_EIGHTH, SOLTIME_A, CHORD_CONTINUE, WHITE_KEY },
{41,0,0,0,0,0, BEAT_110, 0, 0, DURATION_EIGHTH, SOLTIME_B, CHORD_CONTINUE, WHITE_KEY },
{31,0,0,0,0,0, BEAT_110, 0, 0, DURATION_EIGHTH, SOLTIME_B, CHORD_END, WHITE_KEY },
{34,0,0,0,0,0, BEAT_110, 0, 0, DURATION_EIGHTH, SOLTIME_B, 0, WHITE_KEY },
{36,0,0,0,0,0, BEAT_110, 0, 0, DURATION_EIGHTH, SOLTIME_B, 0, WHITE_KEY },
{38,0,0,0,0,0, BEAT_110, 0, 0, DURATION_EIGHTH, SOLTIME_B, 0, WHITE_KEY },
{41,0,0,0,0,0, BEAT_110, 0, 0, DURATION_EIGHTH, SOLTIME_B, 0, WHITE_KEY },

//Measure 4

{42,0,0,0,0,0, BEAT_110, 0, 0, DURATION_EIGHTH, SOLTIME_A, CHORD_START, WHITE_KEY },
{24,0,0,0,0,0, BEAT_110, 0, 0, DURATION_EIGHTH, SOLTIME_A, CHORD_CONTINUE, WHITE_KEY },
{42,0,0,0,0,0, BEAT_110, 0, 0, DURATION_EIGHTH, SOLTIME_B, CHORD_CONTINUE, WHITE_KEY },
{31,0,0,0,0,0, BEAT_110, 0, 0, DURATION_EIGHTH, SOLTIME_B, CHORD_END, WHITE_KEY },
{0,0,1,1,0,0, BEAT_110, 0, 0, DURATION_EIGHTH, SOLTIME_B, 0, BLACK_KEY },
{38,0,0,0,0,0, BEAT_110, 0, 0, DURATION_EIGHTH, SOLTIME_B, 0, WHITE_KEY },
{0,1,0,0,0,1, BEAT_110, 0, 0, DURATION_EIGHTH, SOLTIME_B, 0, BLACK_KEY },
{42,0,0,0,0,0, BEAT_110, 0, 0, DURATION_EIGHTH, SOLTIME_B, 0, WHITE_KEY },
//Measure 5
{43,0,0,0,0,0, BEAT_110, 0, 0, DURATION_EIGHTH, SOLTIME_A, CHORD_START, WHITE_KEY },
{27,0,0,0,0,0, BEAT_110, 0, 0, DURATION_EIGHTH, SOLTIME_A, CHORD_CONTINUE, WHITE_KEY },
{43,0,0,0,0,0, BEAT_110, 0, 0, DURATION_EIGHTH, SOLTIME_B, CHORD_CONTINUE, WHITE_KEY },
{31,0,0,0,0,0, BEAT_110, 0, 0, DURATION_EIGHTH, SOLTIME_B, CHORD_END, WHITE_KEY },
{34,0,0,0,0,0, BEAT_110, 0, 0, DURATION_EIGHTH, SOLTIME_B, 0, WHITE_KEY },
{38,0,0,0,0,0, BEAT_110, 0, 0, DURATION_EIGHTH, SOLTIME_B, 0, WHITE_KEY },
{45,0,0,0,0,0, BEAT_110, 0, 0, DURATION_EIGHTH, SOLTIME_B, 0, WHITE_KEY },
{0,1,0,1,0,0, BEAT_110, 0, 0, DURATION_EIGHTH, SOLTIME_B, 0, BLACK_KEY },

//Measure 6
{45,0,0,0,0,0, BEAT_110, 0, 0, DURATION_EIGHTH, SOLTIME_B, 0, WHITE_KEY },
{0,1,0,1,0,0, BEAT_110, 0, 0, DURATION_EIGHTH, SOLTIME_B, 0, BLACK_KEY },
{45,0,0,0,0,0, BEAT_110, 0, 0, DURATION_EIGHTH, SOLTIME_B,0, WHITE_KEY },
{42,0,0,0,0,0, BEAT_110, 0, 0, DURATION_EIGHTH, SOLTIME_B, 0, WHITE_KEY },
{44,0,0,0,0,0, BEAT_110, 0, 0, DURATION_EIGHTH, SOLTIME_B, 0, WHITE_KEY },
{43,0,0,0,0,0, BEAT_110, 0, 0, DURATION_EIGHTH, SOLTIME_B, 0, WHITE_KEY },

//Measure 7
{41,0,0,0,0,0, BEAT_110, 0, 0, DURATION_EIGHTH, SOLTIME_A, CHORD_START, WHITE_KEY },
{27,0,0,0,0,0, BEAT_110, 0, 0, DURATION_EIGHTH, SOLTIME_A, CHORD_END, WHITE_KEY },
{41,0,0,0,0,0, BEAT_110, 0, 0, DURATION_EIGHTH, SOLTIME_B, CHORD_START, WHITE_KEY },

{31,0,0,0,0,0, BEAT_110, 0, 0, DURATION_EIGHTH, SOLTIME_B, CHORD_END, WHITE_KEY },
{34,0,0,0,0,0, BEAT_110, 0, 0, DURATION_EIGHTH, SOLTIME_B, 0, WHITE_KEY },
{36,0,0,0,0,0, BEAT_110, 0, 0, DURATION_EIGHTH, SOLTIME_B, 0, WHITE_KEY },
{38,0,0,0,0,0, BEAT_110, 0, 0, DURATION_EIGHTH, SOLTIME_B, 0, WHITE_KEY },
{41,0,0,0,0,0, BEAT_110, 0, 0, DURATION_EIGHTH, SOLTIME_B, 0, WHITE_KEY },

//Measure 8
{42,0,0,0,0,0, BEAT_110, 0, 0, DURATION_EIGHTH, SOLTIME_A, CHORD_START, WHITE_KEY },
{24,0,0,0,0,0, BEAT_110, 0, 0, DURATION_EIGHTH, SOLTIME_A, CHORD_END, WHITE_KEY },
{42,0,0,0,0,0, BEAT_110, 0, 0, DURATION_EIGHTH, SOLTIME_B, CHORD_START, WHITE_KEY },
{31,0,0,0,0,0, BEAT_110, 0, 0, DURATION_EIGHTH, SOLTIME_B, CHORD_END, WHITE_KEY },
{0,0,1,1,0,0, BEAT_110, 0, 0, DURATION_EIGHTH, SOLTIME_B, 0, BLACK_KEY },
{37,0,0,0,0,0, BEAT_110, 0, 0, DURATION_EIGHTH, SOLTIME_B, 0, WHITE_KEY },
{43,0,0,0,0,0, BEAT_110, 0, 0, DURATION_EIGHTH, SOLTIME_B, 0, WHITE_KEY },
{42,0,0,0,0,0, BEAT_110, 0, 0, DURATION_EIGHTH, SOLTIME_B, 0, WHITE_KEY },

//Coding of the first four measures of Saints

//Measure 1
{0,0,0,0,0,0, BEAT_120, 0, 0, DURATION_QUARTER, SOLTIME_B, 0, WHITE_KEY },
{36,0,0,0,0,0, BEAT_120, 0, 0, DURATION_QUARTER, SOLTIME_B, 0, WHITE_KEY },
{38,0,0,0,0,0, BEAT_120, 0, 0, DURATION_QUARTER, SOLTIME_B, 0, WHITE_KEY },
{39,0,0,0,0,0, BEAT_120, 0, 0, DURATION_QUARTER, SOLTIME_B, 0, WHITE_KEY },

//Measure 2
{40,0,0,0,0,0, BEAT_120, 0, 0, DURATION_QUARTER, SOLTIME_B, 0, WHITE_KEY },
{33,0,0,0,0,0, BEAT_120, 0, 0, DURATION_QUARTER, SOLTIME_B, CHORD_START, WHITE_KEY },
{31,0,0,0,0,0, BEAT_120, 0, 0, DURATION_QUARTER, SOLTIME_B, CHORD_CONTINUE, WHITE_KEY },
{29,0,0,0,0,0, BEAT_120, 0, 0, DURATION_QUARTER, SOLTIME_B, CHORD_END, WHITE_KEY },
{33,0,0,0,0,0, BEAT_120, 0, 0, DURATION_QUARTER, SOLTIME_B, CHORD_START, WHITE_KEY },
{31,0,0,0,0,0, BEAT_120, 0, 0, DURATION_QUARTER, SOLTIME_B, CHORD_CONTINUE, WHITE_KEY },

{29,0,0,0,0,0, BEAT_120, 0, 0, DURATION_QUARTER, SOLTIME_B, CHORD_END,
WHITE_KEY },
{33,0,0,0,0,0, BEAT_120, 0, 0, DURATION_QUARTER, SOLTIME_B, CHORD_START,
WHITE_KEY },
{31,0,0,0,0,0, BEAT_120, 0, 0, DURATION_QUARTER, SOLTIME_B, CHORD_CONTINUE,
WHITE_KEY },
{29,0,0,0,0,0, BEAT_120, 0, 0, DURATION_QUARTER, SOLTIME_B, CHORD_END,
WHITE_KEY },

//Measure 3
{33,0,0,0,0,0, BEAT_120, 0, 0, DURATION_QUARTER, SOLTIME_B, CHORD_START,
WHITE_KEY },
{31,0,0,0,0,0, BEAT_120, 0, 0, DURATION_QUARTER, SOLTIME_B, CHORD_CONTINUE,
WHITE_KEY },
{29,0,0,0,0,0, BEAT_120, 0, 0, DURATION_QUARTER, SOLTIME_B, CHORD_END,
WHITE_KEY },
{36,0,0,0,0,0, BEAT_120, 0, 0, DURATION_QUARTER, SOLTIME_B, 0, WHITE_KEY },
{38,0,0,0,0,0, BEAT_120, 0, 0, DURATION_QUARTER, SOLTIME_B, 0, WHITE_KEY },
{39,0,0,0,0,0, BEAT_120, 0, 0, DURATION_QUARTER, SOLTIME_B, 0, WHITE_KEY },

//Measure 4
{40,0,0,0,0,0, BEAT_120, 0, 0, DURATION_QUARTER, SOLTIME_B, 0, WHITE_KEY },
{33,0,0,0,0,0, BEAT_120, 0, 0, DURATION_QUARTER, SOLTIME_B, CHORD_START,
WHITE_KEY },
{31,0,0,0,0,0, BEAT_120, 0, 0, DURATION_QUARTER, SOLTIME_B, CHORD_CONTINUE,
WHITE_KEY },
{29,0,0,0,0,0, BEAT_120, 0, 0, DURATION_QUARTER, SOLTIME_B, CHORD_END,
WHITE_KEY },
{33,0,0,0,0,0, BEAT_120, 0, 0, DURATION_QUARTER, SOLTIME_B, CHORD_START,
WHITE_KEY },
{31,0,0,0,0,0, BEAT_120, 0, 0, DURATION_QUARTER, SOLTIME_B, CHORD_CONTINUE,
WHITE_KEY },
{29,0,0,0,0,0, BEAT_120, 0, 0, DURATION_QUARTER, SOLTIME_B, CHORD_END,
WHITE_KEY },
{33,0,0,0,0,0, BEAT_120, 0, 0, DURATION_QUARTER, SOLTIME_B, CHORD_START,
WHITE_KEY },
{31,0,0,0,0,0, BEAT_120, 0, 0, DURATION_QUARTER, SOLTIME_B, CHORD_CONTINUE,
WHITE_KEY },
{29,0,0,0,0,0, BEAT_120, 0, 0, DURATION_QUARTER, SOLTIME_B, CHORD_END,
WHITE_KEY },

```
{SONG_END, 0, 0, 0, 0, 0, 0, 0, 0, 0, 0, WHITE_KEY}
    };

        //This is the end of the coding for the scales and parts of songs Elise and Saints.
        // The Robo diagnostic sketch continues below

    struct  myNote * pSong = Elise;

    void setup()      //the setup routine runs once when the reset switch is pressed
                      //initialize the digital pins as outputs or inputs
        {
    pSong = Elise;

    int i = START_FIRST_KEY;          //Reset Mosfets of keys 0 to 4
    while(i <= END_FIRST_KEY)  {
    pinMode(i, OUTPUT);
    digitalWrite(i, LOW);
    i++;
            }
    i = START_BLACK_KEY;              //Reset Mosfets of keys 5 to 9
    while(i <= END_BLACK_KEY)  {
    pinMode(i, OUTPUT);
    digitalWrite(i, LOW);
     i++;
      }
    i = START_CONFIG_KEY;            //Reset Mosfets of keys 10 to 17
    while(i <= END_CONFIG_KEY)  {
    pinMode(i, OUTPUT);
    digitalWrite(i, LOW);
    i++;
            }
    i = START_WHITE_KEY;             //Reset Mosfets of keys 20 to 53
    while(i <= END_WHITE_KEY)  {
    pinMode(i, OUTPUT);
    digitalWrite(i, LOW);
    i++;
            }
     {
    pinMode(18, OUTPUT);
    pinMode(19, OUTPUT);
     }
```

```
}
void playTune(struct myNote * pTune) {

byte Port1 = pTune->Port;        // Select a Port
int Soltime= pTune->Soltime;     // Select one of 4 setting for the solenoids

if(Port1 == SONG_END) {          // End the song when Port 255 is detected
pSong = pTune;
return;
}

if(pTune->Sustain == 1) {        // Turns on the sustain feature on Port 18
digitalWrite(18, HIGH);
}

if(pTune->Sustain == 0) {        //Turns off the sustain feature on Port 18
digitalWrite(18, LOW);
}

if(pTune->Volume == 1) {         // Turns the volume feature to low on Port 19
digitalWrite(19, HIGH);
}

if(pTune->Volume == 0) {         //Turns the volume feature to full on Port 19
digitalWrite(19, LOW);
}

int beat = pTune->Beat ;                   // Establishes the beat time of the song (millisecs)
beat = beat * beatMult[pTune->Duration]/4;  // Establishes the 5 durations of the notes
                                            // from full to one sixteenth based on the beat (millisecs)
int durMS =  beat  * Soltime/4 ;           // Establishes the amount of time that the solenoids
                                            // are energized .25,.50,.75 or 1.0 of beat time (millisecs)
if(pTune->BlackKey == HIGH) {              //Creates the binary code for the ports of the black notes
digitalWrite(5, pTune->blackStateP5);
digitalWrite(6, pTune->blackStateP6);
digitalWrite(7, pTune->blackStateP7);
digitalWrite(8, pTune->blackStateP8);
digitalWrite(9, pTune->blackStateP9);
} else {
if(Port1) {
digitalWrite(Port1, HIGH);     // Execute command HIGH for the designated white or black note
```

209

```
        }                           // Energize the solenoids for time duration durMs
}
struct myNote * pChordTune = pTune;

if((pChordTune->Chord == CHORD_START) || (pChordTune->Chord ==
CHORD_CONTINUE)) {
pChordTune++;                   // Combine individual notes into chords
 playTune(pChordTune);
 }

if((pTune->Chord == CHORD_END) || (pTune->Chord == 0)) {
delay (durMS);                  // Determines the length of time that the
}                               // Solenoid is energized. One delay per chord

if(pTune->BlackKey == HIGH) {       //Turn off the black keys (ports 5 to 9)
int i = START_BLACK_KEY;         // after the end of the durMS delay
while(i <= END_BLACK_KEY) {
pinMode(i, OUTPUT);
digitalWrite(i, LOW);
  i++;
    }
}else {
int i = START_FIRST_KEY;         //Turn off the white keys (ports 0 to 4)
while(i <= END_FIRST_KEY) {      // after the end of the durMS delay
pinMode(i, OUTPUT);
digitalWrite(i, LOW);
i++;
 }
i = START_CONFIG_KEY;            //Turn off the white keys (ports 10 to 17)
while(i <= END_CONFIG_KEY) {     // after the end of the durMS delay
pinMode(i, OUTPUT);
digitalWrite(i, LOW);
i++;
 }
i = START_WHITE_KEY;             //Turn off the white keys (ports 20 to 53)
while(i <= END_WHITE_KEY) {      // after the end of the durMS delay

pinMode(i, OUTPUT);
digitalWrite(i, LOW);
i++;
 }
```

210

```
        }
        // Now wait out the beat time (Duration of the note)

        if((pTune->Chord == CHORD_END) || (pTune->Chord == 0)) {
        pTune++;
        pSong = pTune;

        delay (beat-durMS);        //After the completion of the note or chord, select the next note

        //Serial.begin(9600);        // Activate the Serial Monitor
        //int n = (beat);
        //Serial.println (n) ;
          }
        }
        void loop() // the loop routine runs over and over
        {
                if(pSong->Port == SONG_END) {
                        pSong = Elise;
                        delay(2000);
                }
        playTune(pSong);
        }
```

Shown above is all the software necessary to play the scales of the black and white keys, the first eight measures of "Elise" and four measures of "Saints," as well as the 20 combinations of note durations and solenoid durations. With this sketch we will perform various diagnostic tasks using the three techniques mentioned at the beginning of the chapter.

Building the Diagnostic and Music Sketches

Unfortunately, there is no easy way to build an Arduino sketch with the code shown above except by typing in all eight pages. The good news is that when the Robo code is needed for another sketch such as "MPP from Book Saints 2.0" or "MPP from Book Elise 2.0", it can be copied and pasted into the new sketch. My plan is to have a website for this book — modernplayerpiano.com — in which I will provide a free download of the first chapter and of the complete Robo sketch shown above. That will make it much easier to download it into your PC error-free. For now, we will type it into a new Arduino sketch and save it as a new file called "MPP Elise Diagnostic 10.0".

After typing it in (there is enough repetition to make Edit's copy and paste feature very useful), verify it (same as compiling it) to correct any errors. Missing commas and semicolons are worth checking first. Checking for curly braces that are not properly paired is also worth doing. The Arduino IDE software helps here, as when you place your pointer right after one of the curly braces it draws a blue box around the other half of the pair.

No matter how careful you are, there will be errors. The ones in the song are easy to find by starting at the beginning of the song with a few lines that compile correctly and adding about 10 lines at a time and compiling each time until you find the error. Make sure that all the "#defines" compile correctly before going on to the songs. Note that when you open the new sketch in which to type the eight pages of the sketch, the "void setup" and "void loop" commands are already on the page. To compile the #define sections and the coding of the scales and songs these commands are necessary. Later, after the diagnostic sketch Robo has been typed in, these commands can be deleted since they are included in Robo.

To retrieve stored files I use the up arrow just below "tools." I find that it works better than the "Files" from the Arduino IDE. Notice also that when a long sketch is compiled for the first time it might take several minutes. Sometimes, when the sketch is modified and the words "build options changed, rebuilding all" appear at the bottom of the page, the compilation also takes several minutes. However, after these "builds" have been completed the compiling process takes less than a minute. Its progress shows on the green bar at the bottom right of the page.

After the sketch "MPP Elise Diagnostic 10.0" is made error-free and compiled, only the music code needs to be uploaded to the Mega and the scales and songs can be played. You should have uploaded about 3362 bytes of code (1294 for the scales and the songs and 2068 for the sketch). This leaves more than 256,000 free bytes in the Mega to store music. The notes and the music take about 35 seconds to play. At that rate, the 256,000 bytes of memory in the Mega can store about 115 minutes worth of music in one upload.

To recap the building of the music and diagnostic sketches:

1. Open a new sketch which includes the "void set-up" and "void loop" commands.

2. Type in the "#defines" in groups and verify/compile the sketch after typing each group.

3. Type in the scales and songs in groups and compile after each group.

4. Carefully type in the last 3 pages of the Robo code without compiling the sketch until you reach the end.

5. Compile the entire sketch. You may now upload the sketch into the Mega 2560, check out the operation of the keys and play some music.

Summary of Chapter 15

The diagnostic sketch that we developed in this chapter is a combination of several routines to test the operation of our mini-robots and a portion of the two songs that we have previously coded. The platform for these routines is the Robo sketch. This sketch is called "MPP Elise Diagnostic 10.0".

Using this sketch and the diagnostic tools and techniques described in the next chapter, it is possible to test all the features of the player piano as well as playing a few measures of music.

CHAPTER 16

Diagnostic Capabilities

Slow Motion Operation

For all diagnostic testing, we will use the sketch "MPP Elise Diagnostic 10.0" described in the previous chapter. Before going into slow motion, listen to the scales and the songs for obvious mistakes. If you find an error, measure at what point the error occurs in the song using a watch with a second hand. By comparing this time with the total time of the song, it is possible to narrow the error location to within one or two measures.

A more useful diagnosis tool is to slow the beat down to the point where you can follow the sheet music of the song easily while it is playing on the keyboard. Performing this operation is simply a matter of changing the number of milliseconds that follow the beat that is being used for the song. For example, in the #define section, after BEAT_110 (for "Elise"), we find the number 550. Change that number to, say, 5500 and compile the sketch again and upload it. Like magic, the same song will play at a pace ten times slower. You can adjust the number again to another value with which you would like to experiment. Compile and upload each time.

At the slow beat it is fairly easy to follow the notes in the sheet music but it is even easier if you coded the music in the two-step method where the port numbers are recorded next to the note. Starting from middle C (port # 36, key 20), it is a good idea to label every fifth keyboard key with the port number on a piece of masking tape. It will really help if you want to make notes about some questionable solenoids while playing the scales.

While the song is playing in slow motion, you may like to check out the effect of the soltime percentage and make sure that it is coded to your liking. A simple test is to replace the value of the number after the most used soltime, namely B. In the #define list, just put a 2 (50%) or a 1 (25%) instead of the 3 after #define SOLTIME_B. Compile/upload again and you will see and hear the effect of this change.

Selecting Specific Sections of the Song

Another useful technique to check for a specific problem is to select a few measures of the song and play them over and over. With this diagnostic you could listen to, say, three measures at the beginning of "Elise" by "commenting out" the scales before Elise with a /* at the beginning and */ at the end of the scales. Then with another pair of /* and */ after the measures of interest to the end of the song. Doing this will cause the sketch to cycle through the three measures continuously and ignore the rest of the notes. In the three measures of "Elise" shown in the example below, we comment out the first and third measures so that only the second measure is played repeatedly.

```
//Measure 1
/*{45,0,0,0,0,0, BEAT_110, 0, 0, DURATION_EIGHTH, SOLTIME_B, 0, WHITE_KEY },
*/{0,1,0,1,0,0, BEAT_110, 0, 0, DURATION_EIGHTH, SOLTIME_B, 0, BLACK_KEY },

//Measure 2
{45,0,0,0,0,0, BEAT_110, 0, 0, DURATION_EIGHTH, SOLTIME_B, 0, WHITE_KEY },
{0,1,0,1,0,0, BEAT_110, 0, 0, DURATION_EIGHTH, SOLTIME_B, 0, BLACK_KEY },
{45,0,0,0,0,0, BEAT_110, 0, 0, DURATION_EIGHTH, SOLTIME_B, 0, WHITE_KEY },
{42,0,0,0,0,0, BEAT_110, 0, 0, DURATION_EIGHTH, SOLTIME_B, 0, WHITE_KEY },
{44,0,0,0,0,0, BEAT_110, 0, 0, DURATION_EIGHTH, SOLTIME_B, 0, WHITE_KEY },
{43,0,0,0,0,0, BEAT_110, 0, 0, DURATION_EIGHTH, SOLTIME_B, 0, WHITE_KEY },
```

```
//Measure 3
/*{41,0,0,0,0,0,  BEAT_110,  0,  0,  DURATION_EIGHTH,  SOLTIME_A,  CHORD_START,
WHITE_KEY },
{27,0,0,0,0,0,  BEAT_110,  0,  0,  DURATION_EIGHTH,  SOLTIME_A,  CHORD_CONTINUE,
WHITE_KEY },
{41,0,0,0,0,0,  BEAT_110,  0,  0,  DURATION_EIGHTH,  SOLTIME_B,  CHORD_CONTINUE,
WHITE_KEY },
{31,0,0,0,0,0, BEAT_110, 0, 0, DURATION_EIGHTH, SOLTIME_B, CHORD_END, WHITE_KEY
},
{34,0,0,0,0,0, BEAT_110, 0, 0, DURATION_EIGHTH, SOLTIME_B, 0, WHITE_KEY },
{36,0,0,0,0,0, BEAT_110, 0, 0, DURATION_EIGHTH, SOLTIME_B, 0, WHITE_KEY },
{38,0,0,0,0,0, BEAT_110, 0, 0, DURATION_EIGHTH, SOLTIME_B, 0, WHITE_KEY },
{41,0,0,0,0,0, BEAT_110, 0, 0, DURATION_EIGHTH, SOLTIME_B, 0, WHITE_KEY },
*/
```

This technique can be used for any song, not just the diagnostic sketch. In the following example we use the song "MPP Elise from Book 2.0". Let us say that you want to do a careful check of the notes in measures 14, 15 and 16. These are the measures with the miniature treble clef that shifts the notes from the bass staff to the treble staff for these three measures. Place a /* in front of the first line of Elise and a */ in front of measure 14. Then you place an opening /* in front of the first line of measure 17 and a closing */ before the curly brace of "Song End...." Now, instead of cycling through the three measures of the song every 45 seconds, the cycling takes place every 5 seconds and will only include the measures of interest.

Now return the #define list to its original condition. One at a time, we will check out the operation and the effect of activating the sustain and the low volume features of the Robo sketch. After #define SUSTAIN_OFF and #define VOLUME_FULL simply replace the numeral 0 (the normal setting) with a 1. Compile and upload again and you will hear the effect of these features in an actual song. If you want to customize the diagnostic sketch or the songs by inserting some sustain or low volume, go to the note coding of the measures and replace the "0"'s for the notes that you select with "1"'s.

Checking other Features of the Robo Sketch

Chords are also easy to check at very low speeds. You can make sure that the correct solenoids are all activated together just by observing their action. Four measures of "Saints" were included in the diagnostic sketch for this purpose. When coding chords, we often divide a half note, for example, into two quarter notes to match them with the other quarter notes in the chord shown in the other staff. We then place an "A" for the soltime of the first quarter note to make it operate like a half note (two quarter notes linked together without interruption).

Such a technique can also be checked out visually. In fact, if you replace the "A"'s in the cord with "B"'s, you will see an interruption in the solenoid operation. Isolate the four measures of "Saints" with pairs of /* and */ in front and back of the measures to cycle through this code which has numerous cords. Remember that Robo applies the soltime code located next to END_CHORD to the entire chord.

The tempo, sustain and volume level are all under the control of the music coder of the song because very few instructions are provided in the sheet music. Arrangements (modifications) of the song are also possible: I have heard "Saints" played like Boogie Woogie! But be aware that to make changes of this magnitude requires the talents of a true musician.

The last operation worth checking with the diagnostic is the correct interpretation of the 20 different combinations of note duration (beat) and the duration of the time that the solenoid is energized. For example, when the beat is 120 BPM we know that the duration of a quarter note is 500ms (with a 4/4 formula). This section of the diagnostic plays five different notes with 4 different Soltimes one at a time. Only an error in the software could cause these notes to play incorrectly but it is a good idea to tune your ear to these sounds. Notice how quickly sixteenth notes are played and notice also that we inserted a pause after the notes with A soltimes. Without it, the note with the A soltime would combine with the next note without discernable interruption.

The Serial Monitor

The second method of diagnosing possible problems or just to determine exactly what Robo is doing is by using the Serial Monitor. It is a piece of software that is part of the Arduino IDE which you downloaded on your PC. The Serial Monitor is activated by selecting its icon (top right-hand corner of the screen). Click on it when a board such as the Mega is connected to the PC via the USB cable. The built-in function "Serial.println ()" will send a line of print back to your PC telling you what is happening each time a note is played. This will all be clear with an example. The routine that we have inserted just before "void loop()" near the end of the Robo code consists of the following three lines of code.

```
Serial.begin(9600);      //Start the Serial Monitor
int n=(beat-durMS);
Serial.println (n);      //Print the results on the PC screen
```

The first line starts the serial monitor program, the second line tells the monitor which data we are interested in (in this case, n equals the last delay after the solenoid has been released for each note) and the third line tells the monitor to "print" the information on the PC. This group of three lines can be moved to various locations in the sketch. All that needs to be done is to copy and paste the three lines in the new location and to put the name of the variable to be tested in the parenthesis.

A good location for the Serial Monitor code is near the end of the Robo sketch after "delay (beat-durMS)" We can leave the three lines of code that activate the Serial Monitor in this location after we are finished with the diagnostic work by simply commenting out the three lines with double slashes (//). To explain its operation we will delete the three double slashes, run the Serial Monitor and see what it tells us.

First, we must decide what we want to know. Our plan is to make a chart with all the values of the important delays that determine the duration of the notes and of the solenoid operations (these values are calculated during the operation of the sketch). We have the perfect routine in the diagnostic sketch for this demanding exercise: the worst-case scenario of the twenty combinations of note types and soltimes for 5 solenoids (white keys 20 to 24). The routine covers every type of note from full to one-sixteenth and every solenoid activation from 100% to 25% (A,B,C, and D). We also added three lines of code to quantify the values of the "blip" notes (the first 2 lines of code are slight pauses before the blip note is activated).

The Serial Monitor Chart

We will run the Serial Monitor with the following names in the parenthesis on the second line: "Port1" (the port number); "beat" (the duration of the note in milliseconds); "durMS" (the duration of the soltime in milliseconds) and "beat-durMS" (the amount of time before the start of the next note after the solenoid has been released, in milliseconds). All notes will be activated at 120 BPM to keep the arithmetic simple. The chart with the values obtained by the Serial Monitor (S.M.) is shown below in Fig 16.1.

Let us see what the chart tells us. The first column shows what we coded in the diagnostic sketch namely the port number and the four soltimes for each note to be tested. The five groups of five notes start with full notes, then half notes, then quarter notes, then eighth notes and finally sixteenth notes. Notice that the second note in each group is a rest note. That was done to isolate the notes with a soltime A from the next note. Without it, the two notes would sound like a single longer note. At the end, two pauses were coded before a blip note with a very fast 300 BPM which is about as fast as the solenoids can operate reliably.

Port No. & Soltime	SERIAL MONITOR			
	Port1	beat	durMS	beat-durMS
36-A (Full)	36	2000	2000	0
36-A	0	2000	2000	0
36-B	36	2000	1500	500
36-C	36	2000	1000	1000
36-D	36	2000	500	1500
37-A (Half)	37	1000	1000	0
37-A	0	1000	1000	0
37-B	37	1000	750	250
37-C	37	1000	500	500
37-D	37	1000	250	750
38-A (1/4)	38	500	500	0
38-A	0	500	500	0
38-B	38	500	375	125
38-C	38	500	250	250
38-D	38	500	125	375
39-A (1/8)	39	250	250	0
39-A	0	250	250	0
39-B	39	250	187	63
39-C	39	250	125	125
39-D	39	250	62	188
40-A (1/16)	40	125	125	0
40-A	0	125	125	0
40-B	40	125	93	32
40-C	40	125	62	63
40-D	40	125	31	94
41-B (1/16)	0	125	93	32
41-B	0	125	93	32
41-B	41	50	37	13

Fig 16.1 – The Serial Monitor Results

The next four columns show the consolidated results returned by the Serial Monitor and printed on the PC screen, with each test yielding one column of data. For the test where n is called "Port1", we received a column of port numbers. Notice that for these tests, port "0" was programmed for the rest notes. When n is called "beat" the Serial Monitor returned a column of durations in milliseconds. The first five being 2000ms for the duration of full notes when the soltime is A and the #define of the beat is 120 BPM (500ms for a quarter note). Under the same conditions, a half note lasts 1000ms, which is the duration of the next five notes. As the notes get shorter, we see faster and faster times down to 125ms for a sixteenth note.

The next column headed "durMS", is the amount of time that the solenoid is activated according to the soltime letter from A to D (100% down to 25%). As we can see from the results soltime A is always four times as long as soltime D. When a note has a soltime condition called soltime A, we would expect that the solenoid would be energized for the entire duration of the beat and the results prove that it is. The last column is called Beat-durMS. This is a second delay that occurs to make sure that the beat of the note runs through completion when the solenoid is activated for less than 100%. For example, on the third line we see that a normal soltime B is attached to full note: middle C (port 36). The solenoid is activated for 1500ms but another delay of 500ms (beat-durMS) has to play out before this full note can be completed and the next note started. That is exactly what the Robo sketch is programmed to do.

Finally, we have three lines showing the results of coding a very short (blip) note. The first two lines are only used to provide a short pause before note 41 is played. It is coded with a very short beat of 50ms and a normal soltime of B. As the results indicate, the solenoid is active for 37ms. If a soltime of C had been coded, the solenoid would be active for 25ms (such a short duration might cause erratic operation in some solenoids). Whatever the soltime, the beat of the note is still 50ms.

The next section on oscilloscope images will provide some visual effects to reinforce the results obtained in this chart. But there can be no doubt that Robo performs all the specified functions exactly as required to reproduce the sheet music faithfully.

Oscilloscope Images of the Notes

My oscilloscope has an interesting musical history. I was working on an electric boat and an electric airplane project (My Electric Boats, Netcam Publishing) when I decided that it was time to upgrade my old oscilloscope. I found one on Craigslist. The seller was a musician who invited me to check it out at his apartment (which turned out to be more like his den!). He told me that he did not know much about oscilloscopes but that he was tying to synthesize (harmonize) some of his music. His girlfriend had bought him the oscilloscope for his birthday. The whole idea turned out badly. The synthesizing project did not work, the girlfriend left him and now, he needed money! It worked out well for me—I bought a very good scope for about half the price of a new one. See the image of the scope below.

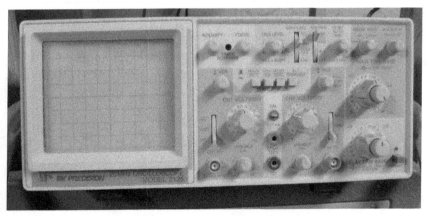

Photo 16.1 – My Oscilloscope

Oscilloscope screens are difficult to photograph, so I'll do my best to draw pictures of the images obtained from the screen. The oscilloscope works like a heart monitor which has a horizontal trace going across the screen with vertical blips indicating the patient's pulse. In our images, time is also represented by the horizontal trace and the closing and opening of the solenoids are represented by the vertical line created by the 5 volt output of the computer ports.

The knobs on the front of the scope are used to adjust the speed of the trace and the height of the pulses so that the image on the screen can be interpreted readily. But there is a lot more to scoping than merely attaching a probe to an electrical connector and twisting a few knobs. The routine running in the computer which generates the traces has to be suitable for display on an oscilloscope. The repetition rate must be fairly rapid and the action being scoped must have a single purpose. For example, if we were to scope the gate level of Mosfet 41 while 45 seconds worth of "Fur Elise" was playing, we would learn nothing. The repeat rate would be too slow to show the trace clearly and the signal from port 41 would show all the notes 41 in the entire song not just the one of interest.

Instead, we will isolate measure 3 of "Fur Elise" by commenting out the sections of the song ahead of measure 3 as well as the sections after measure 3. We will also reduce the 5-second delay at the end of the song to 100ms and comment out the last three notes of the measure so that the routine will cycle fast enough to produce a bright trace.

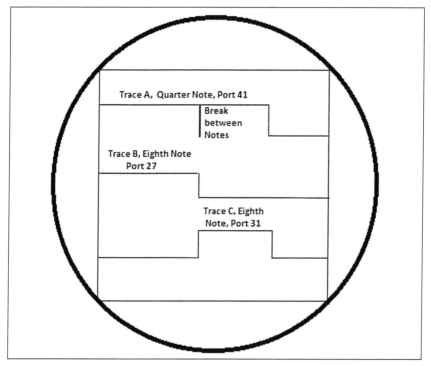

Fig 16.2 – Traces of the First Chord of Elise, Measure 3

We will use two probes: the first one will go to the gate of the Mosfet that drives the solenoid attached to port 41. The number 41 quarter note is divided into two eighth notes which are played as 2 two-note chords paired first, with an eighth note from port 27 and then with an eighth note from port 31. As we see in the diagram above, the top trace shows that the two number 41 eighth notes make a single quarter note because the first eighth note has a soltime A while the second eighth note has a soltime B. Trace A rises to 5 volts at the start of the picture and the trace remains high for about an inch before the break and ¾ of an inch after the break.

Trace B is obtained with the second probe which is attached to the gate of the Mosfet which drive solenoid 27. It also rises to 5 volts at the start of the picture but it only travels about 1 inch before returning to ground (0 volts). Using this same second probe, we will then attach it to the gate of the Mosfet that drives solenoid 31. By doing this swap we obtain Trace C. It starts at ground level for about 1 inch and then, at the break, it goes high to 5 volts for a distance of 3/4 inch and returns to ground in synchronism with Trace A.

The meaning of the composite image of the three traces shown in Fig 16.2 tells us that half of the travel of quarter note 41 consists of a chord with note 27, while for the other half of the travel it turns into a chord with note 31. The shorter ¾ inch distance that Traces A and C travel in the second half of the traces is due to their soltime B notation. For the first half of the chord their soltime A notation caused them to travel a full inch.

The second oscilloscope image (Fig 16.3) provides the answer to an interesting question that can only be answered with the use of an oscilloscope. Namely how long does it take the Mega computer to link the two eighth notes together and turn them into a quarter-note? The image below shows an expanded view of the break between the two eighth notes shown in Trace A. We know that the Serial Monitor determined that the time period was 0 milliseconds so we can assume that it must be a short period of time even though the Mega goes through several hundred calculations during this time.

Expanding the picture of the break about a hundred times tells us that the break in the middle of the trace measures approximately 400 microseconds (.4 ms). This short break is the amount of time that the Mega spent generating the second of the two eighth-notes. It tells us convincingly that two eighth notes can be turned into a quarter note by using the "soltime A" notation in the first note. The reason that it works is that the solenoid cannot react to a pulse lasting less than one millisecond. It would take at least 10 milliseconds to have any effect on the operation of the solenoid.

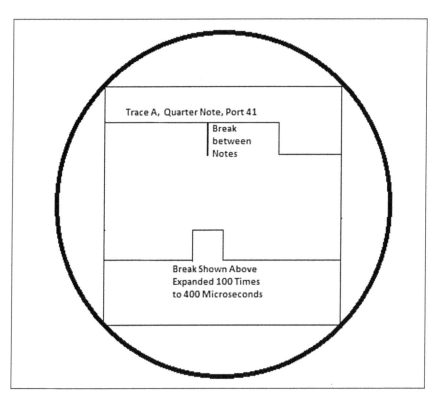

Trace A, Quarter Note, Port 41

Break
between
Notes

Break Shown Above
Expanded 100 Times
to 400 Microseconds

Fig 16.3 – Zoom of the Break Between Two Eighth Notes Linked Together

Review of the Three Diagnostic Methods

In this chapter, we discussed three ways to determine how well Robo operates and we provided tools to detect and repair any suspicious problem. We assembled a diagnostic sketch with features such as playing the scales of the white and black notes and playing a few measures of "Saints" and "Elise". We showed how the normal speed of the music can be reduced to slow motion. So slow, in fact, that the notes being played can be followed on the sheet by a musically illiterate person like me.

We also inserted the Serial Monitor into the diagnostic code. It provided time durations in milliseconds for all the important functions that the Robo sketch performs. The *piece-de-resistance* is a chart of the duration time of 20 notes generated with all combinations of note types and solenoid time durations.

Finally, we used the oscilloscope to "scope" the operation of notes played as chords. We made an important determination: we measured the amount of time that the Mega spends processing the data needed to form a chord. We found that it is so fast that the solenoids do not have time to react during the 400 microsecond time period.

Conclusion

If you are like me, you have learned a lot about music and C++ programming. I had a good foundation in electronics and computer hardware but given how fast those areas tend to progress, it was a good opportunity to bring myself somewhat up to date. This project is for hobbyists and do-it-yourselfers who not only want to build something interesting, but also want to learn something new while doing it. I think that the combination of music, electronics and computers certainly provides ample opportunity for learning new, state-of-the-art technology. We only scratched the surface of course, but it might be enough to discover an area of interest for a lifetime of exciting endeavors.

This is a good place to end this project but for those who want to do more the possibilities are limitless. The mini-robots certainly could be improved to sound less robotic and quieter. Simplifying the coding by scanning the sheet music and producing lines of code for the notes would be a challenging project. Designing a player piano shield for the Mega 2560 would greatly simplify the wiring. But I don't want to usurp all this fun. I will stop here and leave these ideas for another generation of doers.

Glossary of Technical and Musical Terms

Ampere: a measure of the current flowing in an electrical wire

Binary Code: a numbering system that uses only 1's and 0's

Bit: the 1's and 0's in the binary code

Bus: a conductor wire to which several others are connected to form a ground bus or a 12-volt bus

Byte: a series of 8 bits

C and C++: programming languages

Coaxial Cable: an inner conductor surrounded by an insulating layer and a shield to restrict signal leakage and used mainly to transmit video signals

Countersinking: drilling an angular hole which will accept a flat headed screw

Decoder: an electronic device capable of generating a unique output from a coded input

Distributor: a rotating electrical device capable of connecting an input to various outputs

Electromagnetic Coil: a wire winding carrying an electric current which creates a magnetic flux that generates a mechanical force

Etymology: the study of the origin of words and how their meaning has changed over time

Integer: a whole number, not a fraction

Integrated Circuit (also known as an "IC" or a "Chip"): an electronic device made up of a large number of transistors capable of performing computer functions such as "And" and "Or"

Inverter: a device used to reverse the polarity of a signal. For example, if the input signal to the inverter goes from ground to +5 volts, its output will go from + 5 volts to ground

Jig: a device used to help machine a part precisely. On this project we use one jig to locate the mounting holes of the solenoids and another to slice the Styrofoam washers accurately

Jumper: a wire with clips on each end to facilitate making a quick electrical connection

Grommet: a rubber washer which is inserted in a hole in order to insulate the wires that run through the hole from the metallic edges of the chassis

Lands: the wire equivalents embedded in the printed circuit boards

Lock-nut: an additional locking nut which prevents the original nut from loosening

Logic Board or P.C. Board: an electronic circuit board containing integrated circuits and other electronic devices

Marginal Checking: in this project, testing the operation of the solenoids to make sure that they operate at a lower than the specified voltage

Microprocessor: a computer processor in a single integrated circuit chip

Millivolt: one thousandth of a volt

Mosfet: electronic switching device used to, among other things, turn solenoids on and off. It has 3 terminals: on the left is the gate that turns the switch on and off, the circuit to be activated is connected to the middle terminal (drain) and to the right terminal (source) which is ground in our circuits

Musical Symbols: such as notes, staffs, measures, ledger lines, clefs, tempo, beat, accidentals, beams, ties and slurs, chords, metronome, sustain, as described in Chapter 4.

Nomenclature: a system of names or terms

Octal: numbering system using the base of 8

Ohm: a unit of resistance in an electrical circuit

Ohmeter: a meter to measure resistance, usually part of a multimeter that can also measure voltage and current

Ohm's Law: Volts = amps x resistance (in ohms)

Ports, Output Ports: the computer connections which provide an output signals from the microprocessor. On this project, the signals are used to drive the solenoids

Relay: electrical switching device to turn on/off, start/stop or reverse the direction of a motor or circuit

Sketch: a program for an Arduino computer; the list of instructions that activate the computer

Shield: a PC board designed specifically to be plugged in an Arduino computer to perform a given function such as driving robots

Shunt: a device inserted in an electrical circuit to measure current flow

Solenoid: in this project, the magnetic activator (robot) to depress the keys

Stand-off: a plastic spacer, plastic tube

Sustain: in the musical context, a continuation of the sound of a note as it fades after the key has been released

Toggle: to switch back and forth between two modes of operation

Transistor: a semi-conductor device used to switch or amplify electronic signals. It is the basic building block of integrated circuits.

TTL and DTL Logic: classes of digital circuits built from diodes and transistors

Volt: one volt is the voltage across a one ohm resistor when one ampere is flowing through it.

Watt: power developed by one amp of current multiplied by one volt

Wire-nut: an electrical device used to connect several wires together